THE REAL ME
Lifestyles of Soccer's Top Stars

GW00602681

Bob Hayes
and
Alex Henderson

BLAKE

Published by Blake Publishing Ltd,
3 Bramber Court, 2 Bramber Road, London W14 9PB, England

First published in Great Britain in 1995

ISBN 1 85782 141 6

British Library Cataloguing-in-Publication Data:
A catalogue record for this book is available from
the British Library.

Typeset by Pearl Graphics, Hemel Hempstead

Printed in England by
Clays Ltd, St Ives plc

1 3 5 7 9 10 8 6 4 2

CONTENTS

CONTENTS

F O R E W O R D

Football is still the most beautiful game of all . . . although you could be forgiven for disputing that statement this season. The headlines seem to have been dominated by the darker side of the game – bung inquiries, bribery probes, Eric Cantona's attack on a supporter, the rising number of yellow and red cards... the list goes on. But don't be fooled into thinking that it is now a game without finesse, fair play and a great deal of fun.

Soccer has changed a lot over the years since I used to lace up my boots for Manchester United and Northern Ireland. We now have the Premiership, regular football on Sundays and Mondays, as well as some European cup ties on Thursdays. Oh, and the wages are a bit better than in my day.

But some things never change in this great game of ours – team spirit, the fun, the undying loyalty of the supporters and the dedication of players giving their best come Saturday afternoon (or Sunday afternoon, or Monday evening, or Thursday evening etcetera... !)

And another thing that is still very much part of the game is the contribution of players to the public. Players are often criticised for being too distant from their fans – and too big for their boots.

Sure, there are a few footballers who are a little aloof. Just like there are when it comes to solicitors, actors, civil servants, journalists... and any other job you'd care to name. But, take it from me, the huge majority of footballers give a hell of a lot back to the fans. They sign autographs, they answer fans' letters, they open fêtes – they do what they can with the spare time they have.

And they are more than ready to tell the fans something about themselves – and what goes on behind the scenes in football.

The highs, the lows and the laughs.

The LifeStyle column in *The Sun* has consistently given an insight into these sides of the game to fans of different clubs all over the country. Not just the superstars but the players of the less-publicised clubs, the referees, the managers, the chairmen ... in fact, all sides of soccer.

I, like so many people in the game, have been more than happy to contribute. I have always enjoyed reading about the stars of this great game of ours – and I'm sure you will too.

George Best, 1995.

ACKNOWLEDGEMENTS

People often surprise you in life – and soccer stars are no exception. You see a hard-working, grim-faced footballer tearing all over the pitch, putting in tackle after bone-jarring tackle. He has a stare that can turn you to stone. But that is the image – not the real man. Away from the heat of the game, he is a completely different person.

With the help of the players, the LifeStyle column in *The Sun* has given an insight into the many sides of the stars of soccer. Their favourite moments, their worst moments, their funny episodes. And, as we have found, they are happy to share them with the people who matter the most in the game – the supporters.

It has been our privilege to come into contact with stars from all parts of the game. They have many demands on their hectic lives but they have found the time to contribute to LifeStyle over the years. For that we thank them.

Thanks go to *The Sun*'s army of photographers whose pictures make such a huge contribution to the success of *The Sun*.

In *The Real Me* we present the personalities behind the players – including their League and international careers to the end of the 1994-95 Premiership season. Some answers may have been overtaken by the passage of time.

GEORGE BEST

CAREER RECORD:

Lisnasharragh School/Belfast Schoolboys/Cregagh Youth Club/
Manchester United ground staff 1961/Dunstable Town 1974/
Stockport Co 1975/Cork Celtic Jan 1976/Los Angeles Aztecs
Apr-Aug 1976/Fulham Sept 1976/Los Angeles Aztecs May-Aug
1977 & May 1978/Fort Lauderdale Strikers June-Aug 1978 &
Mar-July 1979/Hibernian Nov 1979/San Jose Earthquakes Apr-
Aug 1980 & Mar-Aug 1981/Bournemouth Mar 1983/Brisbane
Lions July 1983.

	Date signed	Seasons	Lge App	Lge Goals
Manchester United	May, 1963	1963-73	361	137
Stockport (loan)	November, 1975	1975	3	2
Fulham	September, 1976	1976-77	42	8
Bournemouth	March, 1983	1983	5	0

Full United record

Football League: 361 (137 goals) ● FA Cup: 46 (21) League
Cup: 25 (9) ● Europe: 34 (11) ● Total: 466 (178)
International career: Northern Ireland (1964-1977) 37 apps 9
goals.

PERSONAL FILE:

Full name: George Best.

Date of birth: May 22, 1946.

Birthplace: Belfast.

Father's job: Richard is a retired shipyard worker.

Parents' sporting achievements: My dad played soccer at
amateur level but my mother was an Irish international hockey
player.

Home: Two-bedroomed flat in Chelsea.

Family: I'm divorced from Angela. We have a son, Calum, who
was born on February 6, 1981.

Brothers and sisters: I have four sisters – Carole, Barbara
and twins Julie and Grace – and a brother, Ian.

Nickname when playing: Tricky.

What was your childhood ambition? The only thing that
I ever wanted to be was a professional footballer.

GEORGE BEST

Who was your boyhood hero? My Belfast neighbour, Mr Harrison. Before we had a telly, and whenever there was football on, I used to smash a ball against his wall until he invited me in.

What was your biggest thrill in life? Being present at the birth of my son.

What was your biggest disappointment in soccer? Missing a penalty at Old Trafford against Chelsea in the early 1970s.

What was your saddest moment in soccer? Losing to West Ham in the 1964 FA Cup semi-final.

Which present-day footballer do you admire most? German midfielder Lothar Matthaeus.

Who is the greatest player there has ever been? Real Madrid legend Alfredo Di Stefano.

What is your biggest regret? I would have liked to have played in an FA Cup Final and the World Cup Finals.

What would you have done if you hadn't become a footballer? Before I went to United at 15, I had just passed my exams to become a printer.

Who is the funniest player you have ever met? Former Old Trafford full-back Shay Brennan. He insists that he made my European Cup Final goal against Benfica because he passed back to keeper Alex Stepney before Stepney cleared it upfield.

What is your best quality? Surviving. It makes me smile every time I read a piece about myself which begins: 'Fallen idol...'

What is your worst? I'm terrible for putting off even the most important things.

Who did you support as a boy? In Belfast it was Glentoran. My grandfather Jock lived right by the ground. I also followed Wolves.

Which were your favourite grounds? Liverpool, Spurs and Chelsea.

Which was your least favourite ground? Sheffield United.

What other sports and hobbies do you enjoy? I like watching American Football, snooker and horse racing. Hobbies are reading, films and quizzes.

GEORGE BEST

What is the most dangerous thing you've ever done?
I once kicked Liverpool hardman Tommy Smith.

What dangerous thing would you most like to attempt?
A parachute jump.

What is your most prized possession? I'm an honorary
patron of a school for handicapped children in Australia. The kids
painted me a special page which they turned into a scrapbook.

Which famous person would you most like to meet?
Nobody. I've already met them all.

What is your most embarrassing moment? Falling
downstairs at Tramp nightclub. I was sober.

FAVOURITE FILE:

TV programme: *Cheers, Fifteen To One* and American
Football.

Pop star: Eric Clapton.

Food: Thai, Chinese and Lebanese.

Drink: Champagne.

Film: *The Sting.*

Film stars: Anthony Hopkins and Rosanna Arquette.

Animal: German Shepherd dog.

Holiday resort: Muscat, the capital of Oman.

TV star: David Jason.

Comedian: Billy Connolly.

CD: Any by Rod Stewart.

Single: 'Living Years' by Mike And The Mechanics.

City: Sydney.

Soap opera: I don't watch them.

A N D Y   C O L E

Season	Club	Lge App	Lge Goals
1989-90	Arsenal	–	–
1990-91	Arsenal	1	–
1991-92	Arsenal	–	–
1991-92	Fulham (loan)	13	3
1991-92	Bristol City (loan)	12	8
1992-93	Bristol City	29	12
1992-93	Newcastle	12	12
1993-94	Newcastle	40	34
1994-95	Newcastle	18	9
1994-95	Manchester United	18	12

Appearances

International: England (1995-) (1 app, 0 goals), Youth, U21, Football League.

PERSONAL FILE:

Full name: Andrew Alexander Cole.

Date of birth: October 15, 1971.

Birthplace: Nottingham.

Brothers and sisters: I have one brother, Desmond, who is a car valet and six sisters: Lorrain and Marva, who are students; Sybil and Jackie, who are housewives; Patsy, who is a waitress; and Joy who is a nurse.

Who was your boyhood hero? Pele – it was every young boy's dream to be him.

How did you discover Newcastle wanted to sign you? I was picking up some some washing from the launderette and when I came out there was a note on my car windscreen. It asked me to report to my Bristol City manager, Russell Osman. I thought I was in trouble over something but he told me Newcastle's £1.75 million bid had been accepted.

What is your biggest disappointment in football? Only getting four games as a substitute for Arsenal. I aimed to prove George Graham was wrong about me – he said I couldn't score goals consistently enough. I scored 24 League and Cup goals in a year at City in a side that struggled. I think my records for Newcastle and United speak for themselves.

A N D Y   C O L E

Which present-day footballers do you admire most?
Ian Wright is a great goalscorer and Paul Gascoigne is just
brilliant.

Who has been the greatest influence on your career?
My mum, my brother and Alan McCarthy. They all pushed me
when I wanted to give up.

What is the oddest piece of training you've ever done?
At Bristol City I had to kick the ball through the high hurdles to
score.

**Your big-money moves have put a lot of pressure on
you — how have you coped?** I have become a better player
for what I have been through – better for the pressure, better
for the criticism. When I signed for Manchester United everyone
said Andy Cole wasn't worth two bob let alone £7 million. It only
made my shoulders broader, my determination greater.

How big a thrill was it to be selected for England?
I always knew my destiny was to play for England. I knew it
when I was 10 years old. Even when I left Arsenal for Bristol
City I knew my future was in the Premier League. I knew
I would come back. Everything I have achieved has been
through hard work.

Was it a shock when United came in for you? I was
shocked that Kevin Keegan was ready to let me go. I would not
have gone anywhere else. I joined the biggest club in England
and one of the mightiest in Europe. When I walked in to meet the
United players there were top-class internationals everywhere.
I was almost star-struck.

**What do you recall of your five-goal show for United in
the 9-0 win over Ipswich?** I tweaked my ligaments and at
half-time the gaffer suggested it might be an idea to call it a day.
But I refused. I had already got two goals and there was no way
I was coming off. I wanted my hat-trick and I was determined to
get it. I had scored plenty of hat-tricks but I had never scored
five before.

Which is your favourite ground? Highbury, because it is so
spacious.

Which is your least favourite? Hartlepool. It is cold, very
windy and has small dressing-rooms.

A N D Y C O L E

Which team did you support as a boy? Nottingham Forest – my hometown club.

What other sports and hobbies do you enjoy? My main hobby is listening to music but I also enjoy basketball, tennis and cricket.

Do you have any superstitions? I put my shorts on last and I always come out of the tunnel last.

Who is your favourite manager? Former Bristol City boss Denis Smith. He believed in me and gave me my big break by paying Arsenal £500,000 for me.

Who do you most admire? American basketball star Magic Johnson. He's a very brave man to come out and tell the world that he's HIV Positive.

FAVOURITE FILE:

TV programme: *Spender*.

Food: Italian or Chinese.

Drink: Guinness and blackcurrant.

Film: *JFK*.

Film stars: Kevin Costner, Denzil Washington.

Holiday spot: Portugal.

TV star: Bill Cosby.

Comedian: Eddie Murphy.

CD: Barry White.

City: London.

Soap operas: *EastEnders, Brookside*.

Soap character: Barry Grant.

WARREN BARTON

Season	Club	Lge App	Lge Goals
1989-90	Maidstone	42	–
1990-91	Wimbledon	37	3
1991-92	Wimbledon	42	1
1992-93	Wimbledon	23	2
1993-94	Wimbledon	39	2
1994-95	Wimbledon	39	2

Appearances

International: England (1995-) (1 app, 0 goals), England B.

PERSONAL FILE:

Full name: Warren Dean Barton.

Date of birth: March 19, 1969.

Birthplace: London.

Father's job: My dad, John, is a courier driver.

Brothers and sisters: An elder sister, Lisa, who is a nursery nurse and an elder brother, John, who is a courier driver.

Nickname: Wazza.

Who was your boyhood hero? Former Arsenal star Liam Brady, a midfield player with great skill.

What has been your biggest thrill in life? Scoring a goal at Anfield. It was a last minute 35-yard free-kick and it helped Arsenal win the title.

What is your saddest moment in soccer? Scoring an own goal in an FA Cup game at Bristol City. We lost the replay and my old Wimbledon boss Peter Withe got the sack.

Which present-day footballer do you admire most? Ray Wilkins. He always enjoys the game.

Who is the greatest player there has ever been? Pele, because he showed the world the skills and thrills of the game.

Who has been the greatest influence on your career? My brother John has always been behind me.

Who has been your toughest opponent? When he was at Southampton, Stuart Gray never gave me any time on the ball.

9

WARREN BARTON

What would you be doing if you weren't a footballer?
I would have tried to be a footballing coach. Before I turned
professional, I worked for a firm of accountants in the City.
I used to get there on a 50cc moped.

**What has been your greatest sporting achievement
outside football?** Running in the cross-country championships
for Essex when I was at school.

Have you ever been rejected by a club? Yes, Watford let
me go when I was 14 and Leyton Orient released me when I was
17. Both told me I was too small. What really hurt was that my
ability was never questioned – it was always my size and weight.
After Orient turned me down I went home and cried. Within six
months of leaving Orient, I put on one and a half stone and grew
five inches. I wanted to prove them wrong. I look on it now as
their loss, not mine. I went into non-league with Redbridge
Forest before Maidstone picked me up and then I joined
Wimbledon.

How did you build yourself up? I used to ride a bike six
miles a day. I also drank gallons of a special drink but I only put
on a few pounds.

**What has been your funniest moment on the football
pitch?** My Wimbledon team-mate Neal Ardley took a corner at
Leeds but, instead of kicking the ball, he kicked the corner
flagstick and the stick whipped back and hit him.

**What has been the oddest piece of training you've
ever done?** One night, just before a big game, the Wimbledon
lads were taken to Paul Raymond's Revue bar in Soho to
celebrate Joe Kinnear becoming manager.

Which team did you support as a boy? Arsenal.

What is your favourite ground? Highbury, because of its
long history.

Which is your least favourite ground? Aldershot. It's in
the middle of a park and there's not much atmosphere.

What other hobbies and sports do you enjoy? Tennis
and relaxing.

**Have you ever been a victim of Wimbledon's Crazy
Gang?** Shortly after I joined Wimbledon, I said after a game that
we were becoming more of a footballing side. A few days later

WARREN BARTON

the lads suddenly stopped in the middle of training, stripped me and threw me into a muddy puddle. I grabbed a training cone and made a run for it – past Princess Di's wedding dress-maker – Elizabeth Emmanuel. I don't know what she thought of it all, especially as I had to pose for pictures with her later – once I was dressed of course.

Who is your favourite sportsman? John McEnroe.

Who is your favourite manager? Before my move to Newcastle, it was my old Wimbledon boss Joe Kinnear because he paid the wages and put me in the team.

How big a thrill was it to join Newcastle? As soon as I spoke to Kevin Keegan I had no hesitation in signing. You don't have to sell Newcastle. It's a great club and I'm really looking forward to the challenge.

Have you any superstitions? I don't wear my shirt until five minutes before the game.

FAVOURITE FILE:

Pop star: Robert Palmer.
Food: Italian.
Film stars: Robert de Niro, Richard Gere and Julia Roberts.
Holiday resort: Tunisia.
TV star: David Jason.
CD: 'Stars' by Simply Red.
City: London.
Soap opera: *Coronation Street.*
Soap character: Jack Duckworth.

Ruddock heads the ball.

NEIL RUDDOCK

Season	Club	Lge App	Lge Goals
1985-86	Millwall	–	–
1985-86	Tottenham	–	–
1986-87	Tottenham	4	0
1987-88	Tottenham	5	0
1988-89	Millwall	2	1
1988-89	Southampton	13	3
1989-90	Southampton	29	3
1990-91	Southampton	35	3
1991-92	Southampton	30	0
1992-93	Tottenham	38	3
1993-94	Liverpool	39	3
1994-95	Liverpool	37	3

Appearances

International: England (1994-) (1 app, 0 goals), Youth, U21.

PERSONAL FILE:

Full name: Neil Ruddock.

Date of birth: May 9, 1968.

Birthplace: Battersea, London.

Father's job: My dad, Ted, is a shopfitter.

Brothers and sisters: Two older brothers – Gary, who is a glazier, and Colin, who is a shopfitter.

Family pets: A Doberman called Chai.

Nickname: Shooster or Razor.

What was your childhood ambition? To play for Tottenham.

Who was your boyhood hero? Sonny McCormick – he was a brilliant Sunday morning footballer – and Pat Van Den Hauwe who still gives 110 per cent.

What have been your biggest thrills in life? Being at the birth of my son Joshua – I was there because I was suspended. And watching my children grow up.

What have been your highs and lows in soccer? Winning the 1995 Coca-Cola Cup has been a big high. The lows? Losing the Zenith Cup final to Nottingham Forest when I was at Spurs and breaking a leg against Liverpool at White Hart Lane – it was only my fifth game for Spurs. After I joined Liverpool, one of the worst moments was my own goal against Spurs when we were leading 1-0. It wasn't a case of wanting the ground to open up and swallow me – I wanted to dig the hole myself.

What has been your biggest disappointment in life?
One of my brother's children dying shortly after birth. I'm glad to say his twin, Max, is a future England centre-back.

Which present-day footballer do you admire most?
Bryan Robson, a bulldog spirit that never knows when it is beaten.

Who is the greatest player there has ever been?
Former Tottenham midfielder Dave Mackay, a true leader in an era when players were men.

Who has been the greatest influence on your career?
My dad, Ted, and my former Southampton team-mate, Jimmy Case. Dad made sure I knew how to handle myself. Jimmy made me believe I could play at the top level – and stop getting into trouble with referees. Jimmy was one of the hardest players in the game but he controlled his temper. He told me never to change my game but to stop getting involved. I owe a lot to Jim. He took me under his wing and brought it home to me just how stupid I was being. He still keeps in touch.

Who has been your toughest opponent? Teddy Sheringham – hard as nails, good in the air and deceptively quick.

What would you be doing if you weren't a footballer?
Doorman at my dad's club.

Have you been rejected by any clubs? Yes – Tramp and Stringfellows!!

Which teams did you support as a boy? Millwall and Spurs.

Which is your favourite ground? White Hart Lane – I met my wife there.

What sports and hobbies do you enjoy? Golf, and chequers on a quiet Sunday.

Who is your favourite sportsman outside football? Ian Botham.

Have you any superstitions? I always follow the Number 10 out of the dressing room and put on my right sock first.

What is your most prized possession? My wife and children.

Who are your favourite football managers? David Pleat, Chris Nicholl and Terry Venables. Also Jim Kelleher, the boss of Fox Sunday, a team I used to play for.

Is there any other sporting dream you would have liked to have achieved? Partnering Ian Botham when he destroyed the Aussies.

What is the funniest thing you have seen on a pitch? My old Spurs team-mate Steve Sedgley celebrating when he scored a goal.

Which world figure do you most admire? Her Majesty The Queen.

FAVOURITE FILE:

TV programme: *Cheers*.
Pop star: R.E.M.
Food: Pie, mash and liquor.
Drink: Perrier water.
Film: *The Sting*.
Film stars: Michael Caine.
Animal: Terry Hurlock.
Resort: Florida.
Comedian: Mike Osman.
Single: 'Losing My Religion' by REM.
CD: *Complete Madness*.
City: London.
Soap opera: *Dallas*.
Soap character: J R Ewing.

JOE ALLON

Season	Club	Lge App	Lge Goals
1984-85	Newcastle	1	–
1985-86	Newcastle	3	1
1986-87	Newcastle	5	1
1987-88	Swansea	32	11
1988-89	Swansea	2	–
1988-89	Hartlepool	21	4
1989-90	Hartlepool	45	18
1990-91	Hartlepool	46	28
1991-92	Chelsea	11	2
1991-92	Port Vale (loan)	6	–
1992-93	Chelsea	3	–
1992-93	Brentford	24	6
1993-94	Brentford	21	13
1993-94	Southend (loan)	3	–
1993-94	Port Vale	4	2
1994-95	Port Vale	26	8

Appearances

International: England Youth.

PERSONAL FILE:

Full name: Joe Allon.

Date of birth: November 12, 1966.

Birthplace: Gateshead.

Home: Three-bed detached house in Washington.

Brothers and sisters: Two brothers: Paul, who owns A & F Taxis in Washington, and Kev, who is a fitter-welder.

Father's job: Frank is a retired miner.

Family pets: A budgie called Joey.

Nickname: The Face.

Who was your boyhood hero? Les McKeown of The Bay City Rollers pop group, because none of the girls in my class fancied footballers – and they all fancied him.

What has been your biggest thrill in life? Backing Ushers Island at 25-1 when it won the Mackeson Gold Cup.

JOE ALLON

What has been your biggest disappointment in life?
The death of my friend and former team-mate, Alan Davies.

What have been your best and worst moments in soccer? Scoring for Newcastle at St James' Park and seeing Hartlepool relegated from Division Two.

Which present-day footballer do you admire most?
Vincent Peter Jones – yes, the Jones boy. For all his knockers, nobody can ever fault his enthusiasm, endeavour or will to win.

Who is the greatest player there has ever been? Bobby Charlton. A Geordie, good with both feet, fine in the air and scored great goals – a bit like me.

What is the strangest thing that's happened to you in a game? It was after a game. A supporter came up to me in the bar and said: 'What was it you went off with at half-time – an injured groin or hamstring?' I found it a bit disconcerting as I actually played the full 90 minutes. It didn't help that we had lost 3-0.

Who do you room with on away trips? At Hartlepool, it was Paul Baker – the neatest, most organised man I have ever met. He used to start getting dressed for games the night before. At Brentford it was Billy Manuel, who talks more than me – asleep or not.

Who has been the greatest influence on your career?
Bryan 'Pop' Robson at Hartlepool, the undisputed king of goal-scorers. He taught me some of his craft and genius.

Have you ever been mistaken for someone else?
During a game, this bloke said I reminded him of Yeats. I said: 'Great – Ron of Liverpool fame?' He replied: 'No, Eddie from *Coronation Street*.'

What is the craziest request you have had from a fan?
A young fellow called Andy Poole requested a picture to use on a birthday cake. I winced when I thought of him eating a cake with my head on it. As it happened, he sent me a photo of the cake afterwards and it was champion.

Who did you support as a boy? Newcastle. I signed for them when I was 14 and fell in love with them.

What other sports do you enjoy? Horse-racing and golf.

J O E   A L L O N

Have you any superstitions? I put my kit on in the same order every game – and I also go out last on to the pitch.

Do you dream of a particular success in another sport? To ride the winner of the Grand National at 500-1 – and to have backed it.

Which player is the best trainer you have seen? I would have to go for Brian Honour at Hartlepool. You would always want to be on his 5-a-side team. With his effort and commitment, you were always on a winner.

How would you describe yourself for a lonely hearts advertisement? Young, rich, good-looking, quiet gentleman. If interested ring Ryan Giggs – not Joe Allon.

FAVOURITE FILE:

TV programme: *Channel 4 Racing.*

Pop star: M People.

Food: My mam Liz's Sunday dinner.

Drink: Lager top.

Films: *The Quiet Man, Uncle Buck.*

Film stars: John Wayne, John Candy.

Holiday spot: Whitley Bay.

TV star: Bruce Forsyth.

Comedian: Bob Monkhouse.

Sports star: Jockey Frankie Dettori.

City: Newcastle.

Soap opera: *Coronation Street.*

Soap character: Hilda Ogden.

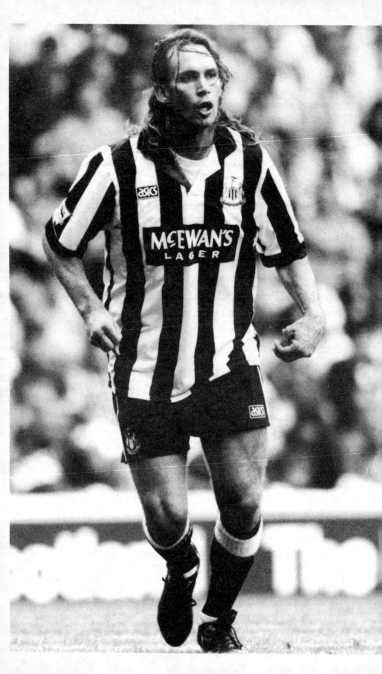

DARREN PEACOCK

Season	Club	Lge App	Lge Goals
1984-85	Newport Co	–	–
1985-86	Newport Co	18	–
1986-87	Newport Co	5	–
1987-88	Newport Co	5	–
1988-89	Hereford	8	–
1989-90	Hereford	36	3
1990-91	Hereford	15	1
1990-91	QPR	19	–
1991-92	QPR	39	1
1992-93	QPR	38	2
1993-94	QPR	30	3
1993-94	Newcastle	9	–
1994-95	Newcastle	35	1

PERSONAL FILE:

Full name: Darren Peacock.

Date of birth: February 3, 1968.

Birthplace: Bristol.

Brothers and sisters: An elder brother, Kevin, who is in the fire service.

Pets: My mum has a poodle called Nick.

Nickname: Hairy.

What was your childhood ambition? To be a professional footballer and to play for Liverpool and England.

Who was your boyhood hero? Kenny Dalglish, he was the star player at the time.

What has been your biggest thrill in life? Playing in the Premier League with QPR and beating Manchester United 4-1 and Liverpool 3-1 away from home. Joining Newcastle – a great club.

What has been your biggest disappointment in life? When Newport County went out of business I was just starting and I did not know if I would find another club. I ended up being the only one in the team to stay in professional football. I was there nearly five years before they went bankrupt. Many a time

DARREN PEACOCK

my pay didn't come through and as an apprentice I needed the money. One cheque bounced six times. When they finally went bust, Colin Addison took me to Hereford.

What has been your saddest moment in soccer? Seeing the footage of the Hillsborough disaster on TV. It was devastating.

Who is the greatest player there has ever been? Pele. He had pace, skill, heading ability and was an example to every player.

Who has been the greatest influence on your career? My mum, Janet. When I was young she went without things herself so she could buy me the best boots.

What would you be doing if you weren't a footballer? When I was younger I did a lot of cycling and won quite a few races so I may have pursued that. More than likely I would have been a builder.

What has been your greatest sporting achievement outside football? Becoming the Bristol and Avon 110m hurdles champion when I was 14.

Have you ever been rejected by a club? I was turned down by Bristol Rovers when I was 16. Former Bournemouth boss Tony Pulis was influential in getting me a trial at Newport after that.

What has been the oddest piece of training you've ever done? When I was an apprentice at Newport, we had to sweep the terraces. We were told to put 100 per cent into it and treat it as a training session!

Which team did you support as a boy? Liverpool.

Which is your favourite ground? Anfield, because of the electric atmosphere and the way the fans appreciate good football.

Which is your least favourite ground? Hartlepool on a cold January afternoon with the wind blowing off the North Sea.

What other sports do you enjoy? Cycling, snooker, tennis, badminton and computer games.

Who is your favourite sportsman outside football? Tennis star John McEnroe, because of his personality and his exceptional skill.

DARREN PEACOCK

Do you have any superstitions? I like to think not but I tend to stick to a routine before a match and I never put my shirt on when I warm up.

Do you play any musical instruments? No, but I would like to learn the saxophone.

Do you dream of a particular success in another sport? I would like to take part in the Tour De France and be King of the Mountains.

FAVOURITE FILE:

TV programme: *Auf Wiedersehen, Pet.*

Pop stars: New Order, Madness, U2.

Food: Spinach, cannelloni.

Drinks: Sparkling water, milk.

Films: *Slap Shot, JFK.*

Film star: Dustin Hoffman.

Holiday resort: Magaluf, with the boys.

Comedian: Tommy Cooper.

CD: *Substance* by New Order.

Cities: Bristol and London.

Soap opera: *Coronation Street.*

Soap character: Jack Duckworth.

LARS BOHINEN

Season	Club	Lge App	Lge Goals
1993-94	Nottingham F	23	1
1994-95	Nottingham F	29	6

Appearances

Overseas clubs: Young Boys Berne.
International: Norway (1989-) (40 apps, 10 goals).

PERSONAL FILE:

Full name: Lars Bohinen.

Date of birth: September 8, 1969.

Birthplace: Vadso, Norway.

Home: Four-bedroomed detached house five minutes from the City Ground.

Cars: A Mazda RX-7 and a BMW 318.

Brothers and sisters: I have an elder sister who works for Coca-Cola in Norway.

Father's job: Journalist.

Nickname: Bo.

Who was your boyhood hero? Michel Platini.

What have been your biggest thrills in soccer? Beating Poland 3-0 away when we qualified for the World Cup. Scoring a goal against England in my first game for Norway in more than a year.

What has been your biggest disappointment in life? I am red/green colour-blind so I could not apply to be a fighter pilot.

What has been your worst moment in soccer? The miserable way Norway performed in the 1994 World Cup Finals.

Which present-day footballer do you admire most? I don't admire any player as I used to when I was younger. I liked the way Jurgen Klinsmann fulfilled all the high expectations people had of him here in Britain.

Who is the greatest player there has ever been? France star Michel Platini, because of his stylish game, his elegance, nonchalance and ability to set up as well as score goals.

LARS BOHINEN

What has been your greatest sporting achievement outside football? Beating my friend Kjetil at squash – I won £50.

Have you ever been rejected by a club? Yes, I went to Vienna for a trial with Rapid, Jan Aage Fjortoft's old club. I wasn't the type of player they were looking for – I ran too much.

Who do you room with on away trips? It used to be Alf Haaland but he snores very loudly – so now I room with anybody but him.

What has been the greatest influence on your career? The three years I spent at Young Boys Berne in Switzerland. It was the lowest point of my career and I learned to deal with pressure, expectations, disappointments and loneliness. It also taught me to distance myself from coaches.

Who is the best trainer you have seen? Nobody has impressed me positively but my former Norway team-mate, Rune Bratseth, must be the most relaxed player ever.

Which celebrity would make a good football manager? John Cleese would make everybody laugh. There is too much seriousness about the game. It means too much to too many people.

What has been the craziest request you have had from a fan? A girl wanted a signed pair of underpants for some reason. I didn't fulfil her dreams.

What would you be doing if you hadn't become a footballer? I would work with languages.

Have you ever needed a kick up the backside in football? After I scored the matchwinner against Italy I got a little big-headed. I was only 20 and couldn't handle the sudden fame. My friends got me down-to-earth quickly. It was an embarrassing experience but very useful.

Which teams did you support as a boy? Juventus and, briefly, Liverpool. Aged six, I ordered a Liverpool kit from a Donald Duck magazine.

How would you describe yourself for a lonely hearts ad? Relaxed, open, interested, egotistical and imaginative.

What other sports and hobbies do you enjoy? Reading,

LARS BOHINEN

computers, tennis, squash, skiing, motorcycling and languages.

What is your most prized possession? My family. I don't value material things as important – they just come and go.

Do you dream of success in another sport? The U.S. Open tennis title.

FAVOURITE FILE:

TV programme: *Have I Got News For You.*

Pop star: Luciano Pavarotti.

Food: Pasta.

Drink: Coke.

Films: *The Godfather* trilogy.

Film stars: Anthony Hopkins, Jeremy Irons.

Holiday spot: Mauritius.

City: Rome.

Comedian: John Cleese.

Sports star: Michel Platini.

Soap Opera: I don't watch any of them – they are all rubbish.

CHRIS BART-WILLIAMS

CAREER RECORD:

Season	Club	Lge App	Lge Goals
1990-91	Leyton Orient	21	2
1991-92	Leyton Orient	15	–
1991-92	Sheffield Wed	15	–
1992-93	Sheffield Wed	34	6
1993-94	Sheffield Wed	37	8
1994-95	Sheffield Wed	38	2

Appearances

International: England Youth, U21, England B.

PERSONAL FILE:

Full name: Christopher Gerald Bart-Williams.

Date of birth: June 16, 1974.

Birthplace: Freetown, Sierra Leone, West Africa. My family moved to Britain when I was four years old and I was brought up in Bounds Green, North London.

Brothers and sisters: A younger brother, Christian, who is studying computing at Barnet College.

Nickname: Shabba.

Who were your boyhood heroes? Pele, Michel Platini and Glenn Hoddle.

What has been your biggest thrill in life? Being chosen for England. I have played for the England Youth, Under-21 and England B sides.

What has been your biggest disappointment? Losing the FA Cup and Coca-Cola Cup finals to Arsenal in the 1992-93 season. It was also disappointing when England Youth lost a World Cup semi-final to Ghana in Australia in 1994.

Which present-day footballer do you admire most? Viv Anderson – the first black player to be picked for England. He taught me a great deal.

What has been your greatest sporting achievement outside football? Playing for my school – St David and St Katherine's in Hornsey, North London. I played football, cricket, tennis and basketball.

Have you ever been rejected by a club? No, I joined

CHRIS BART-WILLIAMS

Leyton Orient when I was 11 after I was spotted by Jimmy Halibone playing for Grasshoppers at Walthamstow. I had just turned 17 when Wednesday bought me for £375,000. It seemed a long way from London but it has proved a great move for me.

How big a difference was it playing in the Premiership? It took me a while to get used to it – you have to think more quickly and move more quickly too. But the manager and senior players helped me out a lot – particularly Paul Williams before he moved to Crystal Palace. People say that I took to playing in the top flight quite quickly. But I must admit that I found the fast pace of the game a big shock.

What did you need to improve when you moved into the Premiership? I have worked hard to improve my heading, tackling and to get into the box more often so I get more chances to score goals.

Who do you room with on away trips? Before his move to Aston Villa, it was Ian Taylor. He slept too much – especially when I wanted to talk to him.

Who has been the greatest influence on your career? All the senior players at Wednesday have helped me. But the biggest influence has been my mum, Edith. She always encouraged me to continue my education when I was at Orient in case I never made it as a professional. I took a YTS course in sports and recreation management.

Who is the best trainer you have seen — and the worst? The best are Roland Nilsson and Mark Bright. They always want to do everything right and give their all. The worst, in my opinion, was Viv Anderson.

What has been the craziest request you have had from a fan? To sign their jeans on their backsides.

Have you ever needed a kick up the backside in football? Trevor Francis did actually give me one. It was at half-time during a Coca-Cola Cup game against Leicester. He told me I was not with it and to pull myself together. He was right.

Which team did you support as a boy? Liverpool. I always admired their football and the way they worked hard.

CHRIS BART-WILLIAMS

How would you describe yourself in a lonely hearts ad? Unpredictable youngster looking for fun.

What other sports do you enjoy? Tennis.

What is your most prized possession? My family and friends, for all the time and support they have given me.

Have you ever dreamed of success in another sport? I would like to win Wimbledon beating Andre Agassi in the final – even though I like him.

FAVOURITE FILE:

TV show: *Fresh Prince Of Bel Air.*

Food: Chicken, rice and peas, African style.

Drink: Orange juice or Guinness punch.

Film: *Jungle Fever.*

Film stars: Wesley Snipes, Jack Nicholson.

Holiday spot: Jamaica.

Comedian: Chris Rock.

Sports star: Chris Eubank.

City: London.

B A R R Y   F R Y

Season	Club	Lge App	Lge Goals
1962-64	Manchester United apprentice	–	–
1964	Bolton	3	1
1965	Luton Town	6	0
1966	Leyton Orient	3	0
1967	Leyton Orient	10	0

Appearances

International: England Schoolboys.

PERSONAL FILE:

Full name: Barry Frank Fry.

Date of birth: April 7, 1945.

Birthplace: Bedford.

Father's job: Frank was a Post Office engineer.

Family: My wife's Kirstine. We have four children – Adam, Frank, Amber and Anna-Marie. I have two children from a previous marriage – Jane and Mark.

Brothers and sisters: None.

Nickname: Basil Brush.

Who was your boyhood hero? Billy Wright, because he was captain of Wolves and England at the time and Wolves were one of the first clubs to appear on TV. He was a tremendous example to all children like myself.

What has been your biggest thrill in life? Finally getting promotion from the GM Vauxhall Conference to the Fourth Division with Barnet.

What has been your biggest disappointment? Only being a has-been-that-never-was as a player. I started as an apprentice at Manchester United with George Best. I was leading scorer in United's reserves for two years but then the gambling bug hit me. I would finish training, jump in the car and go racing at Haydock or York. At night it would be the dogs. One minute I had everything going for me, the next I had nothing and was in non-League. So when I see my own players overdoing it, I have a right go.

B A R R Y   F R Y

What has been your saddest moment in soccer? The day Mick Durham phoned to tell me that his son, Kevin, had died on holiday. He had signed a two-year contract with my club.

Which present-day footballer do you admire most? Bryan Robson. One of the bravest players I've ever seen. I dearly wanted Captain Marvel to pick up the League Championship – and I'm glad he finally did.

Who is the greatest player there has ever been? George Best. A truly brilliant individual with the ability to turn any game whether he was shooting, passing or on one of his famous dribbles when he could leave six or seven defenders helpless.

What is the worst part of your job? Leaving players out of the team.

What was your toughest managerial decision? Parting with Jimmy Greaves, who was my idol, in my first year of management at Barnet.

What has been your biggest managerial mistake? Throwing a glass of whisky (what a waste!) over the chairman and then hitting him. Needless to say, I got the sack the next morning.

What has been your biggest transfer success? Andrew Clarke. One minute he was playing Sunday football and the next he had been sold to Wimbledon for £350,000 – and scoring goals against United, Forest and Everton.

If you won the pools, what would you buy? A TV licence and a tax disc (Ha, ha!).

Which team did you support as a boy? Wolverhampton Wanderers.

Which is your favourite ground? Wembley. I did play there once for England Schoolboys when we beat Scotland 5-3 in 1960 and I scored. In fact I scored five times in six England Schoolboy internationals.

Which is your least favourite ground? Altrincham. I always seem to get a good hiding.

What other sports do you enjoy? Horse-racing and greyhound racing.

B A R R Y   F R Y

What is the most dangerous thing you have done?
Argue with my old chairman, Stan Flashman, at Barnet.

**Which football team do you rate as the best you have
ever seen?** Real Madrid – because of their superb,
entertaining football in which great individual players combined
magnificently as a team.

What is your most prized possession? All my family.

How important is football to you? My missus says I'm very
selfish and should think more about the kids. But she
understands the game is my life. I know one day I'll be out there,
we'll score a goal and I'll jump out of the dugout punching the air
– and drop down dead. But so what? I want to go out on a high
note.

Who would you most like to meet? Franz Beckenbauer.

FAVOURITE FILE:

TV programme: *Saint And Greavsie*.

Pop star: Johnny Mathis.

Drink: White wine and soda.

Film: *Death Wish*.

Film stars: Charles Bronson, Angie Dickinson and Jill
Gascoigne.

Resort: Jersey.

TV star: Michaela Strachan.

Comedian: Norman Wisdom.

CD: *The Best Days Of My Life* by Johnny Mathis.

City: London.

Soap opera: *EastEnders*.

Kerry Dixon scores on his debut.

KERRY DIXON

CAREER RECORD:

Season	Club	Lge App	Lge Goals
1980-81	Reading	39	13
1981-82	Reading	42	12
1982-83	Reading	35	26
1983-84	Chelsea	42	28
1984-85	Chelsea	41	24
1985-86	Chelsea	38	14
1986-87	Chelsea	36	10
1987-88	Chelsea	33	11
1988-89	Chelsea	39	25
1989-90	Chelsea	38	20
1990-91	Chelsea	33	10
1991-92	Chelsea	35	5
1992-93	Southampton	9	2
1992-93	Luton (loan)	17	3
1993-94	Luton	29	9
1994-95	Luton	28	7
1994-95	Millwall	9	4

Appearances

International: England (1985-87) (8 apps, 4 goals), U21.

PERSONAL FILE:

Full name: Kerry Michael Dixon.

Date of birth: July 24, 1961.

Birthplace: Luton.

Father's job: Mike is an electrician.

Brothers and sisters: My sister, Jane, is a hairdresser.

Nickname: At one of my old clubs, it was The Wig – because of a newly-acquired hairstyle.

Who was your boyhood hero? George Best. I was football mad as a kid and he was simply the best.

What has been your biggest thrill? Playing for England, particularly my debut. I scored twice in our 3-1 victory over West Germany at the Aztec Stadium in Mexico.

What has been your biggest disappointment? Losing our Rumbelows Cup semi-final to Sheffield Wednesday during

KERRY DIXON

my Chelsea days. We played so badly and lost 2-0 at home and 3-1 away. I have never played in a major Wembley final. I made it to the FA Cup semi-final with Luton in 1994 but we lost – to Chelsea.

Which present-day footballer do you admire most?
John Barnes. He is outstanding. Liverpool, without Barnes, aren't the same team.

Who is the greatest player there has ever been?
George Best. He was a flair player who could make things happen himself or set it up for others.

Who has been the biggest influence on your career?
My dad. He played 20-30 First Division games for Jimmy Hill's Coventry, and was a reserve in Luton's 1959 FA Cup runners-up side.

What would you be doing if you weren't a footballer?
I didn't become a professional till I was 21. I have a trade as a toolmaker. I did a four-year apprenticeship. It certainly makes you appreciate how lucky you are to be a professional player.

Who have been your toughest opponents? Manchester United's Steve Bruce and Gary Pallister.

Who are the funniest players you have known? At Chelsea we had some right jokers in Dennis Wise, Vinny Jones, Andy Townsend and Joe Allon. They were always getting up to pranks – including swapping car keys on your keyring.

What is the oddest training you've ever done? Every year at Chelsea, we did some pre-season training at Aberystwyth. We had to run up and down the sand dunes and then finish off with a beach run with the tide coming in! You should have seen the non-swimmers go!

Which team did you support as a boy? Luton.

Have you ever been rejected by a club? In my first year in Tottenham's youth team, I was top scorer with about 30 goals but Keith Burkinshaw let me go. He said I lost out on a split-decision by 3-2. In the early 90s, Spurs were ready to pay £1 million for me – but Chelsea sold Gordon Durie for £2 million instead. Rejections like that are tough to take. But it's not the end of the world. My advice to youngsters who are turned away is: keep your heads up – they don't always get it right.

KERRY DIXON

Which is your favourite ground? White Hart Lane. Chelsea always did well there and I always seemed to score.

What other sports and hobbies do you enjoy? I love all sports – squash, golf... anything. I also enjoyed managing a kids' team in Luton – the Bramingham Spitfires. I ran them for 12 to 16-year-olds. One of these youngsters, Jamie Campbell, has played for Luton's first team.

What is the most dangerous thing you have done? Going down a water slide in Tenerife – I'm scared of heights.

Away from football, who are your favourite sportsmen? Ian Botham and Eric Bristow. I like sportsmen who have confidence in their own ability.

Have you any superstitions? I have to follow the same warm-up routine before a game. I chew gum and put on my shinpads and tie-ups in the same order. I also like to come out fourth, carrying a ball.

What are your most prized possessions? My England caps and an inscribed tankard that the boys from Bramingham Spitfires gave me when the side ended.

Which football managers do you admire most? Ron Atkinson and Howard Kendall. They are their own men who have great belief in themselves.

What has been the most embarrassing moment of your life? I once missed a sitter against Norwich. The ball came off the bar and, from just two yards out, I put my shot over the woodwork. Their fans couldn't stop laughing but I had the last laugh when I hit the winner.

Which world figure have you most admired? Mikhail Gorbachev, the Russian leader, for the way he has brought the world together.

FAVOURITE FILE:

TV programme: *Just Good Friends*.

Film: *Revenge*.

Resort: Houston, Texas. I have a lot of family out there.

Single: 'One In A Million' by Larry Graham.

CD: *Can't Slow Down* by Lionel Richie.

ALAN SHEARER

Season	Club	Lge App	Lge Goals
1987-88	Southampton	5	3
1988-89	Southampton	10	–
1989-90	Southampton	26	3
1990-91	Southampton	36	4
1991-92	Southampton	41	13
1992-93	Blackburn R	21	16
1993-94	Blackburn R	40	31
1994-95	Blackburn R	42	34

Appearances

International: England (1992-) (14 app, 5 goals), Youth, U21, England B.

PERSONAL FILE:

Full name: Alan Shearer.

Date of birth: August 13, 1970.

Birthplace: Newcastle.

Father's job: Alan is a sheet-metal worker.

Brothers and sisters: My elder sister, Karen, is a receptionist.

Family pet: A Golden Retriever called Candy.

Nickname: At Southampton it was Smoky, because I used to eat smoky bacon crisps.

Who was your boyhood hero? Kevin Keegan. I used to watch him from the terraces at Newcastle and admire his non-stop running and will to win.

What has been your biggest thrill in life? Scoring a goal on my England debut against France at Wembley was a memorable experience. Then, of course, another big thrill was when Blackburn won the 1994-95 Premiership title.

What has been your biggest disappointment? My grandfather not being alive to see my England debut against France at Wembley. He always took a keen interest in how I was doing.

What has been your saddest moment in soccer? Losing

ALAN SHEARER

to Norwich in the 1992 FA Cup quarter-finals during my time with my old club Southampton.

Which footballer do you most admire? Gary Lineker. He is a great role model for youngsters.

Who is the greatest player there has ever been? Pele. He had the lot.

Who has been the biggest influence on your career? My parents, Alan and Anne. They sacrificed so much for me. I was spotted by a Saints scout up in Newcastle when I was 14. I signed as a schoolboy apprentice when I was 15 and moved down south. But my mum and dad came and saw me as much as possible.

Who has been your toughest opponent? Arsenal's Tony Adams. He is hard and brave.

Who is the funniest player you know? Neil Ruddock. He's full of impressions and gags.

What is the oddest thing that has happened to you at a football ground? At Southampton I once had a bath in soap powder. We were apprentices at the time and there was no bubble bath left. So somebody nipped off to the laundry and came back with soap powder. After I got out I was covered in a rash for days.

Which team did you support as a boy? Newcastle.

Which is your favourite ground? St James' Park. The Newcastle fans are the greatest in the world. I'm pleased to say the supporters at Southampton and Blackburn have really got behind me too.

Which is your least favourite ground? Scarborough on a Tuesday night in January.

What other sports do you enjoy? I like a round of golf – and walking the dog.

What is the most dangerous thing you have done? Getting married..

What dangerous thing would you most like to attempt? A parachute jump. The trouble is, I'm scared of heights.

Who is your favourite sportsman outside football? Nick Faldo. I love the way he can hold his nerve in pressure situations.

A L A N   S H E A R E R

Which world figure have you admired most? Hostage victims Terry Waite and John McCarthy for surviving with courage.

What was your childhood ambition? To be a professional footballer. I was football mad as a kid. I kicked the ball around at school and kicked it around when I got home. If I could I would have played 24 hours a day.

FAVOURITE FILE:

Pop star: Phil Collins.
Food: Pasta.
Drink: Orange juice.
Film: *Another 48 Hours.*
Film star: Patsy Kensit.
Animal: Dog.
Holiday resort: The Algarve.
TV star: Leslie Grantham.
Comedian: Freddie Starr.
CD: *Serious Hits Live.*
Single: 'Another Day In Paradise' by Phil Collins.
City: Newcastle.
Soap opera: *EastEnders.*

ALAN McDONALD

CAREER RECORD:

Season	Club	Lge App	Lge Goals
1981-82	QPR	–	–
1982-83	QPR	–	–
1982-83	Charlton Ath (loan)	9	–
1983-84	QPR	5	–
1984-85	QPR	16	1
1985-86	QPR	42	–
1986-87	QPR	39	4
1987-88	QPR	36	3
1988-89	QPR	30	–
1989-90	QPR	34	–
1990-91	QPR	17	–
1991-92	QPR	28	–
1992-93	QPR	39	–
1993-94	QPR	12	1
1994-95	QPR	39	1

Appearances

International: Northern Ireland (1986-) (47 app, 3 goals), Youth.

PERSONAL FILE:

Full name: Alan McDonald.

Date of birth: October 12, 1963.

Birthplace: Belfast, Northern Ireland.

Father's job: Retired foreman fitter.

Brothers and sisters: Two brothers and a sister. Roy is an insurance broker, Linda works in a laundry and Jim is a transport manager.

Nickname: Macca or Jimmy.

Who was your boyhood hero? I had a few. Jimmy Nicholl, the former Northern Ireland international, lived just 50 yards away and obviously there were George Best and Pat Jennings.

What has been your biggest thrill in football? Playing in the 1986 World Cup finals in Mexico and being captain of Northern Ireland.

What is your biggest disappointment? The death of my youngest brother at 19.

A L A N   M c D O N A L D

What is your saddest moment in soccer? The death of David Bulstrode when he was chairman at QPR. He was a truly nice man.

Which present-day footballer do you admire most? Ray Wilkins. At his age, he puts the rest of us to shame with his attitude and the fact that he's as bald as a coot.

Who is the greatest player you have ever seen? George Best. He has taken so much stick but watching him play was worth ten of anybody else's games.

Who have been the greatest influence on your career? Bill Smith, for persuading me to sign for QPR, and my family for their support through the first few years when I was very homesick.

What would you be doing if you weren't a footballer? Before I joined QPR from school, I fancied going into the Army. But it probably would have been too hard for me.

What has been your greatest sporting achievement outside football? Flying a glider at Kent Gliding Club and living to tell the tale.

Have you ever been rejected by a club? When I was 15 I had two trials with Bolton. They said I would never make a player – and they were right.

What is your funniest moment on a football pitch? When we started pre-season training one year it was a scorcher. We had just finished some very hard running and were knackered. Gary Waddock was trying to be clever and decided to get a drink of water from the sprinkler. Well, the sprinkler head kept turning and Gary broke two of his front teeth. We all creased up laughing.

What is the oddest piece of training you've ever done? When QPR had the Astroturf, it snowed around Christmas so we had to clear the pitch with a gang of prisoners from Wormwood Scrubs.

Which team did you support as a boy? I used to switch from Leeds to Manchester United and then to QPR. But I always supported Glasgow Rangers and an Irish team called Crusaders.

Which is your favourite ground? Old Trafford. I went on

trial twice there and the stadium is superb. It's a shame about the pitch though, otherwise it would be truly amazing.

Which is your least favourite ground? Hillsborough. We once got beaten 7-1 and it's rare for me to be on the winning side.

What other sports do you enjoy? Golf and fishing.

Away from football, who is your favourite sportsman? American basketball star Michael Jordan.

Who is your favourite football manager? Jim Smith. The Bald Eagle throws things, rants and raves but he's a great character and a nice man. Really, all the managers I have had have been good in their own ways.

Do you have any superstitions? If we win, I try to do everything and dress the same for the next match.

What is your most prized possession? My football momentos, because they all have memories. And also the fiver Danny Maddix gave me – that is a sacred note.

Which world figure do you most admire? I would admire the person who invents a legal fitness pill so that we do not have to do any more pre-season training. It is murder.

FAVOURITE FILE:

TV programme: *Just Good Friends*.

Pop stars: Jeff Lynne and Bryan Adams.

Food: Anything Italian.

Drink: I like a lager at weekends, otherwise it's a Diet Coke.

Film: Any Spaghetti Western.

Film star: Clint Eastwood.

Animal: Dastardly and Muttley – the dog's laugh kills me.

Resort: Cyprus.

TV star: Bob Monkhouse.

Comedian: Chubby Brown.

CDs: *Reckless* by Bryan Adams and *Out Of The Blue* by ELO.

Book: The Bourne books by Robert Ludlum.

City: Jerusalem.

Soap character: Dirty Den.

Crook evades another challenge.

I A N   C R O O K

Season	Club	Lge App	Lge Goals
1980-81	Tottenham	–	–
1981-82	Tottenham	4	–
1982-83	Tottenham	4	–
1983-84	Tottenham	3	–
1984-85	Tottenham	5	1
1985-86	Tottenham	4	–
1986-87	Norwich City	33	5
1987-88	Norwich City	23	1
1988-89	Norwich City	26	1
1989-90	Norwich City	35	–
1990-91	Norwich City	32	3
1991-92	Norwich City	21	1
1992-93	Norwich City	34	3
1993-94	Norwich City	38	–
1994-95	Norwich City	34	–

Appearances

International: England B.

PERSONAL FILE:

Full name: Ian Stuart Crook.

Date of birth: January 18, 1963.

Birthplace: Romford, Essex.

Family pets: A Doberman called Major.

Nickname: Chippy! It's a long story.

Who was your boyhood hero? I was a West Ham fan so Trevor Brooking was my idol.

What has been your biggest disappointment? Not being at the birth of my first son Sean. I was away at Everton before our first game of the season. I had spoken to Joanne before going to bed and everything was okay. Sean wasn't expected for a week or so. I was woken the next morning to be told I was a father.

What have been your best and worst moments in soccer? Beating Bayern Munich in the UEFA Cup. My abiding memory of playing in the Olympic Stadium was how tiring the whole experience was. The worst was being beaten by Everton in the 1989 FA Cup semi-final. Everyone was so depressed. Then we heard what had happened at Hillsborough and it put everything into perspective.

Which present-day footballer do you admire most?
Paul Gascoigne. Despite everything he's been through he keeps picking himself up and coming back.

Who is the greatest player there has ever been? Pele. There's never been another player with his vision.

What has been your greatest sporting achievement outside football? Winning the Anglian Windows Golf Pairs tournament with my old team-mate Trevor Putney.

Have you ever been rejected by a club? Spurs let me go to Norwich. I joined Tottenham the same week that Ossie Ardiles and Ricky Villa arrived. You could learn so much from them, including Spanish. Glenn Hoddle was without doubt the country's most gifted player. It was a privilege to play alongside him. But, with Glenn, Ossie and Mickey Hazard in the side, there wasn't room for me as well. A lot of what I heard and saw stuck. And the experience of all that has helped me.

What is the strangest thing that has happened to you on the pitch? In one of my first games for Tottenham I came on as sub against Chelsea at Stamford Bridge. I was on my own, 30 yards from the nearest player and I tripped and fell flat on my face. It was the Spurs' fans who laughed the most. I didn't. I was taken off on a stretcher with torn knee ligaments and was out for weeks.

Who do you room with on away trips? Mark Bowen. He moans constantly – even in his sleep!

Who has been the greatest influence on your career?
Mike Walker gave me a second chance which renewed my appetite for the game. And Steve Perryman gave me great advice at Tottenham.

Who is the best trainer you have seen — and the worst? Jerry Goss. Even when he's not in the side he's the best. The worst, in my opinion, is Darren Beckford.

Have you ever been mistaken for someone else? Yes. Trevor Putney. We've got the same nose.

Which celebrity would make a good football manager?
Ronnie Barker. Most players would understand Arkwright from
Open All Hours more than a lot of bosses.

How big a thrill is it to play for England? I count myself
very fortunate that I've got an England B cap. I would be lying if
I said I never wanted to play for the full England side. If that ever
did come along it would be fantastic. It does someone like me a
power of good to see how the likes of Gordon Strachan and Ray
Wilkins have played on at the top of their game past their mid-
30s. It gives everyone in the game hope.

**Have you ever needed a kick up the backside in
football?** I've had too many on and off the field to mention.
Everybody needs them now and again.

What movie would you most like to be in? Any Michael
Douglas film. Because he always ends up with the best girls.

**How would you describe yourself for a lonely hearts
ad?** Homely Sky Sports lover.

What other sports do you enjoy? Golf and snooker.

Who or what irritates you most in football? Manchester
United – because they're too good.

Do you have any superstitions? If we win, I always wear
the same suit for the next game. I don't know what I'm going to
do this season because we've been issued with club jackets.

FAVOURITE FILE:

TV programme: *Only Fools and Horses*.

Pop star: David Bowie.

Food: Cantonese or Thai.

Drink: Lucozade.

Film: *Dirty Rotten Scoundrels*.

Film stars: Demi Moore and Steve Martin.

Holiday spot: Florida's Disneyland.

TV star: David Jason.

CD: *Listen Without Prejudice* by George Michael.

R O B   J O N E S

Season	Club	Lge App	Lge Goals
1987-88	Crewe Alexandra	5	–
1988-89	Crewe Alexandra	19	1
1989-90	Crewe Alexandra	11	–
1990-91	Crewe Alexandra	32	1
1991-92	Crewe Alexandra	8	–
1991-92	Liverpool	28	–
1992-93	Liverpool	30	–
1993-94	Liverpool	38	–
1994-95	Liverpool	33	0

Appearances

International: England (1992-) (8 app, 0 goals), U21.

PERSONAL FILE:

Full name: Robert Marc Jones.

Date of birth: November 5, 1971.

Birthplace: Wrexham.

Cars: A Ford Escort XR3i and a BMW convertible.

Brothers and sisters: A younger sister, Kate.

Nickname: Triggs.

Who was your boyhood hero? Kenny Dalglish.

What has been your biggest disappointment in life?
When England failed to qualify for the World Cup Finals in 1994.
It is the greatest feeling in the world to represent England,
especially when we play at Wembley.

What has been your biggest thrill in football? Signing for
Liverpool. I joined them in 1991 after starting my career with
Crewe Alexandra.

What has been your best moment in soccer? When
Liverpool won the FA Cup in 1992, beating Sunderland 2-0.
Walking up those Wembley steps as a winner to collect my medal
in front of 80,000 people is something I will never forget. It was
a great day and it capped a memorable season for me. Winning
the 1995 Coca-Cola Cup Final against Bolton was a highlight too.

What has been your worst moment in football? The shin
splints injury that kept me out of the game for so long.

R O B   J O N E S

Which present-day footballer do you admire most?
Italy's Roberto Baggio. He is an excellent footballer who looks full of confidence on the ball.

Who is the greatest player you have ever seen? Diego Maradona.

Away from football, what has been your greatest sporting achievement? I was selected for Cheshire cricket team.

Have you ever been rejected by a club? No.

What has been the strangest thing that has happened to you in a game? Not scoring for Liverpool – but I have come very close.

Who do you room with on away trips? Mark Wright. He talks in his sleep.

Who has been the greatest influence on your career? My dad – he has always sent me in the right direction.

Who is the best trainer you have seen — and the worst? The best has to be John Barnes. The worst is our keeper, David James, in five-a-side games.

Have you ever been mistaken for someone else? Yes, for my Liverpool team-mate Nicky Tanner.

What is the craziest request you have had from a fan? A girl once asked me to send her a pair of my boxer shorts.

What would you be doing if you weren't a footballer? I'd like to be a P.E. teacher.

Have you ever needed a kick up the backside in football? Not yet.

Which team did you support as a boy? Liverpool, of course.

How would you describe yourself for a lonely hearts ad? Quite shy, 5ft 10in, blond hair.

What other sports do you enjoy? Golf, tennis and cars. I play golf against John Scales when I'm not too busy. My handicap is 18. I used to enjoy playing basketball at school and I now have a basketball net on the wall above my garage. I mess around out there when I have nothing better on.

R O B   J O N E S

Who or what irritates you most in football? Not scoring yet for Liverpool.

Do you have any superstitions? I always touch the Anfield sign every game before I go out on to the pitch.

What is your most prized possession? My family.

Do you dream of a particular success in another sport? To win the Wimbledon men's tennis title.

FAVOURITE FILE:

TV show: *Play Your Cards Right.*

Pop star: Ice-T.

Food: Pasta.

Drink: Sparkling water.

Film: *Son In Law.*

Film stars: Sharon Stone, Eddie Murphy.

Holiday spot: Cyprus.

Comedian: Rowan Atkinson as Mr Bean.

Sports star: Michael Jordan.

CD: *Ice Cube.*

City: Liverpool.

Soap opera: *Brookside, Coronation Street.*

Soap star: Raquel.

CYRILLE REGIS

Season	Club	Lge App	Lge Goals
1977-78	WBA	34	10
1978-79	WBA	39	13
1979-80	WBA	26	8
1980-81	WBA	38	14
1981-82	WBA	37	17
1982-83	WBA	26	9
1983-84	WBA	30	10
1984-85	WBA	7	1
1984-85	Coventry City	31	5
1985-86	Coventry City	34	5
1986-87	Coventry City	40	12
1987-88	Coventry City	31	10
1988-89	Coventry City	34	7
1989-90	Coventry City	34	4
1990-91	Coventry City	34	4
1991-92	Aston Villa	39	11
1992-93	Aston Villa	13	1
1993-94	Wolves	19	2
1994-95	Wycombe	35	9

Appearances

International: England (1982-88) (5 app, 0 goals), U21 and England B.

PERSONAL FILE:

Full name: Cyrille Regis.

Date of birth: February 9th, 1958.

Birthplace: Maripasoula in the French Guyana. I moved to St Lucia when I was four and then to England.

Brothers and sisters: Two sisters, Nilla and Denise; and brothers, Imbert and David, who is also a professional footballer.

Nickname: C.

What was your childhood ambition? To be a doctor.

Who was your boyhood hero? Former world heavyweight boxing champion Muhammad Ali. The Greatest.

What has been your biggest thrill in life? Becoming a Christian a few years ago. It is a long story but it followed the death of my pal Laurie Cunningham, the former West Brom and England winger who died in a car crash. I started to think about what life really meant.

What has been your saddest moment in soccer? Losing to non-League Sutton United in the FA Cup third round in 1988 when I was with Coventry. We were the holders.

Which present-day footballer do you admire most? Bryan Robson. He's the nearest we have to the complete footballer.

Who is the greatest player there has ever been? Pele. He had the lot.

What's the best part of your job? Winning and scoring goals.

What is the worst? Pre-season training. It is torture.

What would you be doing if you weren't a footballer? An electrician. I did the job for three years when I was playing for non-League Hayes and then Moseley. I have passed all the exams. I stopped when I joined my first League club, West Brom.

If you won a million, what would you buy first? All the things my family wanted.

What is your best quality? I'm punctual.

What is your worst quality? I'm hopeless at cooking.

Which team did you support as a boy? Tottenham. I started when I was about seven and living in North West London.

What is your favourite ground? Old Trafford. The atmosphere is fantastic.

What is your least favourite ground? Highbury. I've never scored a goal there and only won there once.

What other sports do you enjoy? I like playing golf. My handicap? The clubs. I like watching cricket and athletics. I saw my cousin John Regis win World Championship gold in the 4 x 400 metres relay. Kriss Akabusi's final run was terrific.

What is the most dangerous thing you have done? I once got a lift from Derek Statham, my West Brom pal.

What dangerous thing would you most like to attempt? A parachute jump. It looks smashing fun.

CYRILLE REGIS

Are you allergic to anything? Yes, long-distance running.

What is your most prized possession? My FA Cup winner's medal with Coventry in 1987.

Do you play any musical instruments? No, but I'd love to play the saxophone.

Who would you most like to meet? Muhammad Ali – again! I met 'The Greatest' when I was a kid in London. He was the top man then and was at my friend's house. He gave me his autograph – I've still got it somewhere.

Which world figure do you most admire? Nelson Mandela, the South African leader imprisoned for so many years. He has been through so much but has emerged with a lot of dignity.

FAVOURITE FILE:

TV programme: *Cheers*.

Pop star: Aretha Franklin.

Food: Anything Caribbean.

Drink: Tea.

Film: *The Blues Brothers*.

Film stars: Whoopi Goldberg and Michael Douglas.

Resort: St Lucia in the Caribbean.

Comedian: Lenny Henry.

Single: 'Just My Imagination' by The Temptations.

CD: *Aretha Franklin's Greatest Hits*.

I A N   W R I G H T

Season	Club	Lge App	Lge Goals
1985-86	Crystal Palace	32	9
1986-87	Crystal Palace	38	8
1987-88	Crystal Palace	41	20
1988-89	Crystal Palace	42	24
1989-90	Crystal Palace	26	8
1990-91	Crystal Palace	38	15
1991-92	Crystal Palace	8	5
1991-92	Arsenal	30	24
1992-93	Arsenal	31	15
1993-94	Arsenal	39	23
1994-95	Arsenal	31	18

Appearances

International: England (1991-) (20 app, 5 goals).

PERSONAL FILE:

Full name: Ian Edward Wright.

Date of birth: November 3, 1963.

Birthplace: London.

Home: Four-bedroomed detached house in Surrey.

Brothers and sisters: Two brothers, Maurice and Nicky, who are decorators, and a sister, Dionne.

Nickname: Satchmo.

Who was your boyhood hero? QPR and England striker Stan Bowles. If I scored a goal in the school playground I would throw my hands up and pretend I was Stan. He had great ball control, a terrific left foot and bags of flair. And he had that rare ability to look as if he was doing just what he wanted on the pitch. He was a great entertainer and a great player.

What has been your biggest thrill in life? Scoring two goals for Palace in the 1990 FA Cup Final – and playing for England. With Arsenal, the great moments have been our FA Cup, Coca-Cola Cup and European Cup-Winners' Cup triumphs.

What has been your saddest moment in soccer? When I broke a leg for the second time. It looked as though I would miss Palace's FA Cup final against Manchester United but I was on the subs' bench. Luckily for me, I came on to score twice and take the final to a replay.

Which present-day footballer do you admire most?
Cyrille Regis. He was the pioneer for black players and the one I used to look up to. He is still going strong.

Who is the greatest player there has ever been? Pele. His ability, attitude and will-to-win were unbeatable.

What's the best part of your job? Easy – scoring goals.

What is the worst? Losing. It really gets me down.

What would you be doing if you weren't a footballer? I'd be a plasterer.

Who would you most like to be? I am pleased with myself.

What's your best quality? Honesty.

What is your worst? I can be very intolerant.

Which teams did you support as a boy? I followed two – Millwall and Liverpool.

What is your favourite ground? Wembley. It's a magnificent place and gives you a real buzz – especially walking out on to the pitch.

What is your least favourite ground? Millwall's Den. I followed them as a kid but it still doesn't stop the fans barracking me all the time.

Can you remember the first time you teamed up with Mark Bright at Palace? Yes, I had just finished a training session and was caked in mud from head to toe. Brighty walked over and said: 'You look like a mess, you don't even look like a striker.' He said I fell over when I passed, fell when I ran, fell when I had a shot. I could have thought, 'Who the hell are you to tell me what to do?' But he seemed to know what he was talking about. He seemed to have this presence about him.

How big an influence was Mark Bright to you? Over the years, he passed on tips and told me what I was doing wrong. It was always constructive and helpful. Maybe it was because he had been playing with Gary Lineker. He had learned a lot from Gary about how to play, how to act and how to look after yourself.

What other sports do you enjoy? Tennis and basketball.

I A N   W R I G H T

What is the most dangerous thing you have done?
I played at Millwall – and answered the fans back!

What dangerous thing would you most like to attempt?
A parachute jump. It must be a tremendous feeling.

Are you allergic to anything? Cats and dogs. They are not
good for my asthma.

What are your most prized possessions? My England
caps.

Who would you most like to meet? I would have loved to
have met Martin Luther King, the American civil rights leader
who was assassinated.

What job will you do after you stop playing soccer? One
that pays good money.

Which world figure do you most admire? Mikhail
Gorbachev. The Russian leader has helped make the world a
safer place.

FAVOURITE FILE:

TV show: *Cheers.*

Pop stars: Prince, Michael Jackson and James Brown.

Food: Spaghetti Bolognese.

Drink: Tango.

Film: *The Godfather.*

Film star: Robert De Niro.

Animals: Tigers and pumas.

TV star: Ted Danson.

Comedian: Eddie Murphy.

Single: 'Get It Off' by Big Daddy Cane.

CD: *James Brown's Greatest Hits.*

City: Paris.

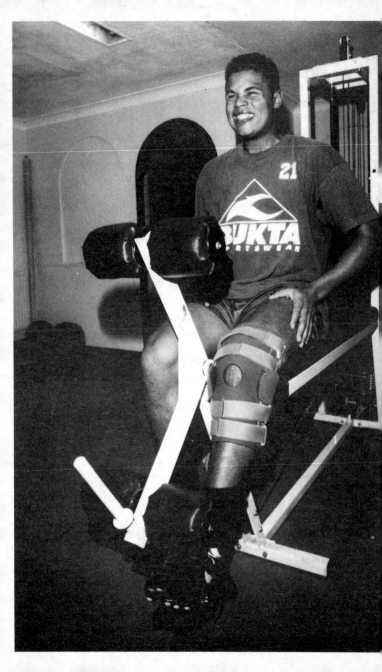

JOHN SALAKO

Season	Club	Lge App	Lge Goals
1986-87	Crystal Palace	4	–
1987-88	Crystal Palace	31	–
1988-89	Crystal Palace	28	0
1989-90	Crystal Palace	17	2
1989-90	Swansea (loan)	13	3
1990-91	Crystal Palace	35	6
1991-92	Crystal Palace	10	2
1992-93	Crystal Palace	13	–
1993-94	Crystal Palace	38	8
1994-95	Crystal Palace	39	4

Appearances

International: England (1991-) (5 app, 0 goals).

PERSONAL FILE:

Full name: John Akin Salako.

Date of birth: February 11, 1969.

Birthplace: Ibadan, Nigeria.

Home: London.

Brothers and sisters: I have three brothers – David, a computer analyst, Paul, a postman and Andrew, a student – and a sister Marie, who has a daughter, Hannah.

Parents' jobs: My mum Jennifer is a teacher. My dad, Albert, was a university professor. He died in 1974.

Family pets: Two cats – Tom and Jerry.

Nickname: Flick.

Who were your boyhood heroes? Pele, Michel Platini and Glenn Hoddle.

What has been your biggest thrill in life? Playing for England at Wembley against the world champions, Germany. The Nigerian FA asked if I'd like to look at their set-up. But I have been brought up as an English lad and it was a natural choice for me to play for England.

Can you recall how you heard England had selected you? I was mowing the lawn on a Sunday afternoon and Alan Smith rang my house. He said Graham Taylor had rung to say I was in the squad for the Australasia tour. I said: 'You're winding me up.' I loved every second of the tour and wished it had never ended.

What has been your biggest disappointment in football? Losing the 1990 FA Cup Final to Manchester United in a replay.

What have been your best moments in soccer? The FA Cup Final, the Zenith Data Systems Final, winning the Division One title and playing for England.

What have been the worst moments? Injuring my knee ligaments twice and being out for two ten-month spells. Three of the four ligaments in my left knee were useless. Two were severed and another was torn. Several specialists said it was too much of a mess in there but a Los Angeles surgeon, Dominic Cisto, performed the operation. If he had turned me down, my career would probably have been over.

Which present-day footballer do you admire most? Roberto Baggio. Brilliant skills and plays the game in the right spirit. A great ambassador for the game.

What is your greatest sporting achievement outside football? I played cricket for Kent County Schools.

Have you ever been rejected by a club? No. Palace has been my one and only club. I joined as a 14-year-old and turned professional at 17.

What is the strangest thing that's happened to you in a game? Playing in goal against Wimbledon when Nigel Martyn was sent off. I made a save that got in a video entitled *100 Great Saves*.

Who do you room with on away trips? Richard Shaw goes to sleep with the TV on. It wakes me up about 3 a.m. so I always end up having to turn it off.

Who has been the greatest influence on your career? My former manager Alan Smith. He has been like a second father to me.

Which player is the best trainer you have seen — and the worst? Ian Wright for his unbelievable enthusiasm – he has a complete love affair with the game. The worst, in my opinion, was Steve Coppell – he cheated because he was the gaffer.

JOHN SALAKO

Have you ever been mistaken for someone else? Yes, the comedian, Gary Wilmot. A few years ago, the fans used to chant his name when I was on the ball.

What is the craziest request you have had from a fan? To sign his forehead. Another fan named his cow after me.

What would you be doing if you weren't a footballer? Presenting a TV show. As a kid, I wanted to be a fighter pilot.

Which team did you support as a boy? Liverpool.

How would you describe yourself for a lonely hearts ad? Tall, dark, handsome, sincere and very funny.

What other sports and hobbies do you enjoy? Golf, snooker, cricket and reading.

Do you dream of a particular success in another sport? To win the US Masters. I would win on the last hole of the last round by one shot – by making a 20ft putt.

Have you ever needed a kick up the backside? Most full-backs I play against seem to think I need one – and they usually give it to me.

FAVOURITE FILE:

TV programme: *Cheers, The Cosby Show.*

Pop star: Prince, Luther Vandross.

Food: Italian.

Drink: Water.

Film: *The Good, The Bad And The Ugly.*

Film stars: Al Pacino, Clint Eastwood.

Sports star: Daley Thompson, Mike Tyson.

CD: *The Bodyguard* soundtrack.

GAVIN PEACOCK

CAREER RECORD:

Season	Club	Lge App	Lge Goals
1984-85	QPR	–	–
1985-86	QPR	–	–
1986-87	QPR	12	1
1987-88	QPR	5	–
1987-88	Gillingham	26	2
1988-89	Gillingham	44	9
1989-90	Bournemouth	41	4
1990-91	Bournemouth	15	4
1990-91	Newcastle	27	7
1991-92	Newcastle	46	16
1992-93	Newcastle	32	12
1993-94	Chelsea	37	8
1994-95	Chelsea	38	4

Appearances

International: England School, Youth, Football League.

PERSONAL FILE:

Name: Gavin Keith Peacock.

Date of birth: November 18, 1967.

Birthplace: Welling, Kent.

Father's job: Keith is reserve team manager at Charlton.

Brothers and sisters: One sister, Lauren, who works for a promotions company.

Nickname: Too many to list.

What was your ambition as a child? To be a professional footballer like my dad, who played for Charlton.

Who was your boyhood hero? I had two – Pele, the greatest, and Kevin Keegan because he epitomised every good thing about football. He made himself into a world-class player with his talent, hard work and dedication.

What has been your biggest disappointment in football? I could not get into QPR's first team regularly. I was 19 and impatient so I turned down the chance of staying in order to establish myself elsewhere.

GAVIN PEACOCK

What is your saddest moment in soccer? The Hillsborough tragedy.

Which present-day footballer do you admire most? Roberto Baggio, a world class player who is capable of the unexpected.

Who is the greatest player there has ever been? Pele... pace, power, skill and an unequalled goalscoring record.

Who has been the greatest influence on your career? My father, Keith. He always set me the right example as a player and then guided and helped me along throughout my career.

When did Christianity become a big part of your life? I always believed in God but I've been an active Christian since I was 19 because of my mum, Lesley. She made a commitment to God and I noticed how she changed; she became happier and more at peace with herself. She used to smoke 30 to 40 cigarettes a day and pray for help. She hasn't touched one since. I also discovered church isn't a boring place full of people just singing hymns. There are a lot of young people like me who have the Christian faith.

Who has been your toughest opponent? Bryan Robson. I was 19 and playing for QPR versus Manchester United. I was up against Robson in his prime – say no more.

What would you be doing if you weren't a footballer? If I hadn't joined QPR at 16, I would have gone on to do my A-Levels at Bexley Grammar School and then gone to university. So now I would probably be on the dole with a Bachelor of Arts degree in my hand.

What is your greatest sporting achievement outside football? Winning the individual award at my school sports day – impressive, eh?

Your family moved to America when you were 11 – did that help your soccer? It was a big change, going to school over there for two years. But, football-wise, I came on a lot and I came back much stronger and more confident. Maybe it helped that I was playing only once or twice a week rather than four or five like some of the kids today, which is ridiculous at an age when their bodies are still developing.

GAVIN PEACOCK

Which team did you support as a boy? Charlton.

What is your favourite ground? Wembley, I played there for England Schoolboys.

What is your least favourite ground? Twerton Park, Bristol Rovers' ground.

What other sports and hobbies do you enjoy? Swimming, golf and reading. I'm also learning Italian.

Is there an unusual food that improves your game? No, I just eat loads of pasta and rice.

Who is your favourite sportsman outside football? Tennis star Andre Agassi.

Who is your favourite football manager? I admire Brian Clough, Ossie Ardiles and Glenn Hoddle for their philosophy on the way the game should be played.

Do you play any musical instruments? I'm learning to play the guitar.

Do you dream of a particular success in another sport? To win an Olympic gold in the 1500 metres.

Which world figure do you most admire? Mother Teresa, for her unbelievable work with the poor in India.

FAVOURITE FILE:

TV programme: *Cheers*.

Pop stars: Phil Collins and Mariah Carey.

Food: Pasta.

Drink: Perrier and lime.

Film: *Chariots Of Fire*.

Film star: Kevin Costner.

Holiday resort: Florida.

CD: *Legend* by Bob Marley and *Emotions* by Mariah Carey.

Book: *Kane And Abel* by Jeffrey Archer.

City: Paris.

Robson with Alex Ferguson.

BRYAN ROBSON

Season	Club	Lge App	Lge Goals
1974-75	WBA	3	2
1975-76	WBA	16	1
1976-77	WBA	23	8
1977-78	WBA	35	3
1978-79	WBA	41	7
1979-80	WBA	34	8
1980-81	WBA	40	10
1981-82	WBA	5	–
1981-82	Manchester United	32	5
1982-83	Manchester United	33	10
1983-84	Manchester United	33	12
1984-85	Manchester United	33	9
1985-86	Manchester United	21	7
1986-87	Manchester United	30	7
1987-88	Manchester United	36	11
1988-89	Manchester United	34	4
1989-90	Manchester United	20	2
1990-91	Manchester United	17	1
1991-92	Manchester United	27	4
1992-93	Manchester United	14	1
1993-94	Manchester United	15	1
1994-95	Middlesbrough	22	1

Appearances

International: England (1980-92) (90 app, 26 goals), England Schools, Youth, U21.

PERSONAL FILE:

Full name: Bryan Robson.

Date of birth: January 11, 1957.

Birthplace: Chester-le-Street, County Durham.

Father's job: My dad Brian is a lorry driver.

Brothers and sisters: An elder sister and two younger brothers. Susan is a secretary. Justin is a shop manager and part-time footballer – he was a professional with Newcastle United but had to quit because of injury. My youngest brother, Gary used to play for West Brom but now plays for Bradford.

BRYAN ROBSON

Family pets: A rabbit called Smokey.

Nickname: Robbo or Pop.

What was your ambition as a child? Like most boys, it was to be a professional footballer.

Who was your boyhood hero? George Best. I love football and there was nobody better.

What has been your biggest thrill in life? On a personal front, it was seeing my children being born. As for football, it is winning trophies.

What has been your biggest disappointment? Missing quite a few games because of injuries.

Which present-day footballer do you admire most? Paul Gascoigne. He has great ability. It is great to see him back for England.

Who is the greatest player there has ever been? Pele. He could do everything with a ball. He could kick with both feet, was a great header of the ball and was so fast.

Who has been the biggest influence on your career? Most of the managers and coaches I have played for have helped in some way.

What would you be doing if you weren't a footballer? A PE teacher.

What is the greatest game you have played in? For entertainment, I think it has to be when my old side, West Brom, beat Manchester United 5-3 at Old Trafford.

What aims do you still have as a player? To win as many things as possible.

Are you as non-stop off the field as you are on it? Yes, I could do with a double.

Have you ever been rejected by a club? No, but when I was at Pelton Roseberry Comprehensive I never got through the county trials.

What is the funniest thing you've seen on a the pitch? Paul Ince going down with cramp in our 1990 FA Cup Final victory against Crystal Palace.

What is the oddest training you've ever done? Going for a bacon sandwich one morning with Brian Kidd.

BRYAN ROBSON

Which team did you support as a boy? Newcastle United.

Would you like to have played for a club abroad? No. I've been very happy staying in England.

What other sports do you enjoy? Horse-racing and golf. I have my own racehorse.

Is there a food that improves your game? Yes, pasta.

Who is your favourite sportsman outside football? Sevvy Ballesteros. I think that he has a great temperament.

Do you have any superstitions? I like to wear the number 7.

What are your most prized possessions? My European Cup-Winners' Cup medal with United and my England caps.

Who is your favourite football manager? I can't judge because I haven't played for all of them.

Which world figure do you most admire? The Queen.

FAVOURITE FILE:

TV programme: *Cheers*.

Pop star: Paul McCartney.

Food: Steak.

Drink: Orange squash.

Film: *The Sting*.

Film star: Clint Eastwood.

Holiday resort: Florida.

Comedian: Bernard Manning.

Single: 'Mull Of Kintyre' by Wings.

City: York.

Soap opera: *Coronation Street*.

Don cautions Sharpe.

P H I L I P   D O N

Commenced refereeing in 1968 (East Yorkshire).
Joined the Football League in 1981 as a linesman.
First refereed in the Football League in 1986.
Highlights: 1992 FA Cup Final (Liverpool 2 Sunderland 0).
　　　　　　1994 World Cup Finals.
　　　　　　1994 European Cup Final (AC Milan 4 Barcelona 0).
　　　　　　1995 Coca-Cola Cup Final (Liverpool 2 Bolton 1).

PERSONAL RECORD:

Full name: Philip Don.

Date of birth: March 10, 1952.

Birthplace: Hull.

Home: Four-bedroomed detached house in West London.

Cars: A Fiat Croma and a Fiat Panda.

Family: I'm married to Judith. We have two children, Nicola and Timothy.

Brothers and sisters: I have two sisters. Susan's a hairdresser, Catherine's a nurse.

Pets: Two goldfish.

What was your childhood ambition? To become a teacher and get as high as I could in my profession. When I started refereeing at 16, my ambition was to referee the FA Cup Final.

What have been your biggest thrills in life? My daughter getting into Oxford University. The second was refereeing my first international – France v Belgium.

What has been your biggest disappointment in life? Not getting on the Football League referees' list at the first attempt.

What has been your saddest moment in soccer? In my third match as a League referee I had to caution seven players and send one off.

Who has been the biggest influence on your career? In refereeing, my fellow members of the Association of Football League Referees and Linesmen who have offered advice over so many years and been prepared to listen.

When did you first become a referee and how long did

it take you to qualify for the Football League? I started in East Yorkshire in 1968 and graduated through the Spartan and Southern Leagues before joining the Football League as a linesman in 1981. I became a referee five years later.

How much training do you do to keep fit? I run between 15 and 25 miles a week. A typical week is – match on Saturday, five-mile runs on Sunday, Tuesday, Wednesday and Thursday, then another match on the next Saturday.

Did you become a referee because you were a football flop? No, I played rugby to county standard and refereed youth soccer on Sundays. When I moved to college, I concentrated on refereeing to supplement my grant.

What has been your greatest achievement as a player? I captained the first XV rugby side at Marist College in Hull for two years and captained the college soccer club.

Does abuse from fans ever bother you? No, as a referee, you hear very little of the individual calls. You hear more as a linesman because you are on the same touchline for 45 minutes.

Had you ever officiated at Wembley before you took charge of the 1992 FA Cup Final between Liverpool and Sunderland? Yes, I was a linesman at the 1976 FA Vase final between Billericay Town and Stamford. I refereed the U15 game between England and West Germany in 1985 and I was the reserve referee for the Leyland DAF Cup final between Tranmere and Bristol Rovers in 1990.

What subjects do you teach at school? I started as a head of PE and also taught geography. At present I teach geography and religious studies.

Which teams did you support as a boy? Hull City and Hull Kingston Rovers.

What are your favourite grounds? Peterborough – because it is the first ground on which I refereed a League match; Norwich – it has excellent hospitality; and Old Trafford – there is such a buzz about the place.

What other sports and hobbies do you enjoy? Athletics, golf, cricket, gardening, cooking and going to the theatre.

Who is your favourite sportsman outside football? Geoffrey Boycott – an outstanding cricketer with total dedication.

PHILIP DON

Do you have any superstitions? I always get things out in the dressing-room in a set way – the three Ps (paper, penny, pencils) and the two Ws (watches and whistles).

Do referees 'switch off' after matches? We don't just forget about it all until our next game. We discuss it all the time and I and other senior referees get calls most days from young officials asking for our advice.

FAVOURITE FILE:

TV programme: Wildlife documentaries.
Pop star: Dire Straits.
Food: Fish, especially salmon.
Drink: Dry white wine.
Film: *Rain Man*.
Film star: Dustin Hoffman.
Resort: Archachon, France.
TV star: John Thaw.
Comedian: Lenny Henry.
CD: *Brothers in Arms* by Dire Straits.
City: Paris.

GARY LINEKER

CAREER RECORD:

Season	Club	Lge App	Lge Goals
1978-79	Leicester	7	1
1979-80	Leicester	19	3
1980-81	Leicester	9	2
1981-82	Leicester	39	17
1982-83	Leicester	40	26
1983-84	Leicester	39	22
1984-85	Leicester	41	24
1985-86	Everton	41	30
1986-87	Barcelona	37	22
1987-88	Barcelona	36	16
1988-89	Barcelona	26	6
1989-90	Tottenham	38	24
1990-91	Tottenham	32	15
1991-92	Tottenham	35	28

Appearances
International: England (1985-92) (80 app, 48 goals), England B.
Overseas club (1992-94): Grampus 8 (Japan).

PERSONAL FILE:

Full name: Gary Winston Lineker.

Date of birth: November 30, 1960.

Birthplace: Leicester.

Dad's job: Barry is a fruiterer on Leicester Market.

Brothers and sisters: One brother, Wayne.

Nickname at club: Links.

What was your ambition as a child? To be a professional footballer or cricketer.

Who was your boyhood hero? Frank Worthington, who played for my team, Leicester City. Not only was he a great player with terrific skill, he was an entertainer.

What has been your biggest thrill in football? Helping Tottenham beat Brian Clough's Nottingham Forest to win the FA Cup in 1991. The disappointment of the day was Paul Gascoigne's knee injury.

GARY LINEKER

What has been your biggest disappointment in life?
My son George's illness.

What has been your saddest moment in soccer? Losing
on penalties to West Germany in our World Cup semi-final in
1990.

Which present-day footballer do you admire most?
Paul Gascoigne, for his immense talent and skill. I hope that he
realises his enormous potential.

Who is the greatest player there has ever been? Pele.
He did it all.

What's the best part of being a striker? That's easy,
scoring goals.

What is the worst? That's easy too, not scoring goals.

What would you be doing if you weren't a footballer?
I would like to have been a cricketer.

Who would you most like to be? A doctor who discovers a
100 per cent cure for leukaemia.

What is your best quality? My laid-back character.

What is your worst? I leave everything to the last minute.

What is your favourite ground? Wembley. I have many
happy memories of the place.

What is your least favourite ground? Villa Park. I cannot
recall ever scoring there.

What other sports do you enjoy? Cricket – I play for the
Lord's Taverners – and golf.

What is your ideal evening out? A meal at a good
restaurant with my wife, Michelle, and some close friends.

What is the most dangerous thing you have done?
I've had to stand in the wall when Stuart Pearce has taken a
free-kick.

Are you allergic to anything? Yes, pollen, I get absolutely
rotten hay-fever.

Did you have any superstitions? I never shot at the goal
during a warm-up. And, to change my luck if I was not scoring,
I would have a haircut.

What are your most prized possessions? My England

GARY LINEKER

caps, my FA Cup winner's medal with Spurs and the Golden Boot award for being top scorer in the 1986 World Cup.

Do you play any musical instruments? No, but I wish I could.

FAVOURITE FILE:

TV programmes: *Have I Got News For You, Clive Anderson Talks Back.*
Pop stars: Elton John, Simply Red's Mick Hucknall.
Food: Japanese.
Drink: Tea.
Film: *The Silence Of The Lambs.*
Film star: Robin Williams.
Holiday resort: Sardinia.
Comedian: The Monty Python team.
Single: 'Holding Back The Tears' by Simply Red.
CD: *Joshua Tree,* by U2.
City: Barcelona.

Bishop (left) shows Paul Ince a clean pair of heels.

IAN BISHOP

Season	Club	Lge App	Lge Goals
1983-84	Everton	1	–
1983-84	Crewe (loan)	4	–
1984-85	Everton	–	–
1984-85	Carlisle United	30	2
1985-86	Carlisle United	36	6
1986-87	Carlisle United	42	3
1987-88	Carlisle United	24	3
1988-89	Bournemouth	44	2
1989-90	Manchester City	19	2
1989-90	West Ham	17	2
1990-91	West Ham	40	4
1991-92	West Ham	41	1
1992-93	West Ham	22	1
1993-94	West Ham	36	1
1994-95	West Ham	29	1

Appearances

International: England B.

PERSONAL FILE:

Full name: Ian William Bishop.

Date of birth: May 29, 1965.

Birthplace: Liverpool.

Father's job: Bob is retired.

Brothers and sisters: Three brothers and three sisters. Mike runs a stud farm in Virginia. Ann lives on an army camp in Cirencester. Anthony, Kenny, Kathleen and Laurice live in Liverpool.

Pet: An Old English Sheepdog called Woodyboyd, after the barman in *Cheers*.

Nickname: Bish – but Martin Allen calls me Yeti.

Who was your boyhood hero? Arsenal's Charlie George. He was an individual with great flair and ability. I was only six when he scored the winner in the 1971 FA Cup Final but it stuck in my mind.

I A N   B I S H O P

What has been your biggest thrill? Finding out my wife Jane was expecting our first baby.

What has been your biggest disappointment in life? My brother, Howard, was killed in Ireland when I was 12 years old. I would have loved him to have seen me playing in the Premiership.

What have been your saddest moments in soccer? Losing an FA Cup semi-final to Nottingham Forest and relegation. I was relegated from the Second to the Fourth in successive seasons with Carlisle, then finished second bottom of the Fourth. I left Manchester City at the bottom and look what I went through in the 1994-95 season. I'm getting a complex.

Which present-day footballers do you admire most? Glenn Hoddle, Ray Wilkins and Neil McNab. There are no others to touch these three for passing ability with either foot.

Who are the greatest players there have ever been? Pele and Johann Cruyff.

What was your favourite subject at school? I got CSE Grade 1 in PE but I also loved art. I drew pictures of Frank McAvennie and Stuart Slater that were raffled off for charity at the Northampton branch of the West Ham supporters' club.

Have you ever been turned down by a club? I was rejected by Aston Villa when I was 15. I already knew I was signing for Everton but, when I received the letter saying I wasn't good enough for Villa, it still hurt.

What has been your funniest moment on a football pitch? At Carlisle, John Halpin took a corner but kicked the flagstick as well. The ball rolled about five yards, a defender came out for it. John tackled him, crossed it and we scored.

What is the oddest training you've ever done? Scott McGarvey, a team-mate at Carlisle, once had to do heading practice on one leg – because his other was in plaster. He wasn't too happy.

Which team did you support as a boy? Arsenal – but I could only see them when they played in Liverpool.

What is your favourite ground? Maine Road has a great atmosphere and, although I only spent six months there, I had a special relationship with the Manchester City fans.

I A N   B I S H O P

What is your least favourite ground? Oldham. I don't remember ever winning there and I even missed a penalty which sent Carlisle down to the Third in the last game of the season.

What are your favourite dressing-rooms? I'll go for Liverpool. It's amusing to read all the little slogans the Liverpool apprentices have written about each other on the benches.

What is the most dangerous thing you have done? One of my teachers put her finger over my mouth while she was reading to the class so I bit it. She screamed and then knuckled me on the head with a large ring.

Who is your favourite sportsman outside football? Baseball and American Football star Bo Jackson. To combine two sports and reach the top in both is an unbelievable achievement.

Who is your favourite football manager? Harry Redknapp. He helped resurrect my career and worked wonders at Bournemouth.

How often do you have your hair cut and do you use shears? Not very often – and only when the person with the shears manages to catch me. A few people have threatened to do it while I am asleep. It is one of my fears.

Which world figure do you most admire? Anyone who takes time out to help people less fortunate than themselves.

FAVOURITE FILE:

TV programme: *Cheers.*
Pop stars: Def Leppard, Del Amitri.
Food: Pasta, or a curry at about 2.30 a.m.
Drink: Guinness.
Film: *The Silence Of The Lambs.*
Film stars: Kim Basinger, the Marx brothers.
Resort: Fleetwood, near Blackpool.
TV stars: David Jason, Ted Danson.
Comedians: Chubby Brown, Bernard Manning.
Single: 'That's Entertainment' by The Jam.
CD: Del Amitri's *Waking Hours.*
Soap star: Sinbad in *Brookside.*

GUY WHITTINGHAM

Season	Club	Lge App	Lge Goals
1989-90	Portsmouth	42	23
1990-91	Portsmouth	37	12
1991-92	Portsmouth	35	11
1992-93	Portsmouth	46	42
1993-94	Aston Villa	18	3
1993-94	Wolves (loan)	13	8
1994-95	Aston Villa	18	3
1994-95	Sheffield Wednesday	21	10

PERSONAL FILE:

Full name: Guy Whittingham.

Date of birth: November 10, 1964.

Birthplace: Evesham in Worcestershire.

Brothers and sisters: An elder sister, Sarah, who is married with four children.

Father's job: My dad, David, is retired.

Family pets: A canary called Asa.

What was your childhood ambition? To play as much sport as possible.

What has been your biggest thrill in life? The birth of my son, Joss. The first 30 seconds when he was blue were a bit scary but after that... total happiness.

What has been your biggest disappointment? Being left on the substitutes' bench for Portsmouth's first FA Cup semi-final against Liverpool.

What has been your saddest moment in soccer? Losing on penalties in the semi-final replay.

Which present — day footballer do you admire most? I can't single one out. There are a lot of players I admire for the dedication they put into the game.

Who has been your toughest opponent Leeds United's Chris Fairclough. He's very strong, quick and good in the air.

GUY WHITTINGHAM

What has been your greatest sporting achievement outside football? An Army Cup winner's medal at cricket – I top-scored with 86 in the final.

Have you ever been rejected by a club? I wrote to both Bristol clubs, Wolves and Swindon as a 15-year-old but never heard from any of them. In 1986 I had trials with Plymouth but it didn't work out. They wanted me to play in reserve games when I was already committed to Army matches.

What would you be doing if you weren't a footballer? Before I joined Portsmouth, I was a PT instructor and corporal in the Army. Pompey paid £450 so I could buy myself out.

Have you an unusual hobby? I took up juggling in 1992 and I'm sure it has helped my concentration and my sharpness on the football pitch. It began when a mate called Mark Bailey came round one day and picked up three apples and started juggling. I had a go and picked it up within five minutes. My wife Martha bought me some juggling balls for my 28th birthday and for Christmas I was given batons. I sometimes take the juggling balls on away trips. It helps while away the time in hotels.

What is your funniest moment on a football pitch? In an Army game, my friend Clint Webbe swung a leg to volley the ball but missed it completely. He landed in a heap and needed treatment from the physio.

What is the oddest training you've ever done? *Dance With Dave* aerobics at HMS Temeraire Navy base in Portsmouth.

What is your favourite ground? Old Trafford is the best stadium I have visited but Portsmouth's Fratton Park has the best surface.

What is your least favourite ground? Oxford's Manor Ground. I never seem to win there.

What other sports do you enjoy? I like most sports and when I was in the Army I did a spot of rock-climbing – but nothing too high. I had a bit of a mishap when we were scaling 100ft cliffs. It was all right going behind the team leaders, who were putting in the pegs but later we had to go first. There were a few close scrapes. I fell once but the rope held and I fell only 15 to 20ft. Despite the accident it was great fun.

GUY WHITTINGHAM

Is there an unusual food that improves your game?
Pasta and rice pudding.

How beneficial has training with top athletics coach Arvell Lowe been? I've gained an awful lot from the extra training. Football is more physical now but the extra workouts have helped me combat that. I have been taught to warm up properly before and after matches. I usually take 15 minutes before the game and then 30 minutes after it which is just as important. I have cut out most junk food and I eat a lot of fresh fruit and pasta and most things the health freaks say you should. Because of that I find myself with extra energy, extra fitness and extra sharpness.

Who are your favourite sportsmen outside football?
Olympic gold medal-winning sprinter Linford Christie and cricketer Ian Botham.

Do you ever dream of success in another sport?
To take part in the Olympic Games.

FAVOURITE FILE:

TV programme: *One Foot In The Grave.*

Food: Pasta.

Drink: Blackcurrant and lemonade.

Holiday spot: West Indies.

Record: 'Dock Of The Bay' by Otis Redding.

Town: Cheltenham.

Soap opera: I hate them.

ROY WEGERLE

Season	Club	Lge App	Lge Goals
1986-87	Chelsea	12	2
1987-88	Chelsea	11	1
1987-88	Swindon (loan)	7	1
1988-89	Luton Town	30	8
1989-90	Luton Town	15	2
1989-90	QPR	19	6
1990-91	QPR	35	18
1991-92	QPR	21	5
1991-92	Blackburn	12	2
1992-93	Blackburn	22	4
1992-93	Coventry	6	0
1993-94	Coventry	21	6
1994-95	Coventry	25	3

Appearances

International: USA (1992-) (21 apps, 2 goals).
Overseas clubs: Tampa Bay Rowdies.

PERSONAL FILE:

Full name: Roy Connon Wegerle.

Date of birth: March 19, 1964.

Birthplace: Pretoria, South Africa.

Father's job: Ernest is a retired civil servant.

Brothers and sisters: I have three elder brothers. Steve is a coach with Rodney Marsh's Tampa Bay Rowdies in Florida. Martin is a chartered accountant, and Geoff is a computer salesman.

Nickname: D'Artagnan is just one of the nicknames my old QPR team-mate Ray Wilkins has given me.

What was your childhood ambition? To be a professional footballer. I lived in South Africa until I was 17 when I gained a soccer scholarship to the University of South Florida.

Who was your boyhood hero? George Best. He had so much flair and was incredible to watch. He was head and shoulders above the rest.

ROY WEGERLE

What has been your biggest thrill in life? When I got to the Littlewoods Cup Final with Luton in 1989. For any English player, it's a dream come true. But for a South African whose only contact with Wembley was through Brian Moore on TV, it was unbelievable. Unfortunately we lost to Forest 3-1.

What has been your saddest moment in soccer? Losing that game. It doesn't hit you until a couple of days later – then it hits you hard.

Which present-day footballer do you admire most? John Barnes. An individual with a very special talent.

Who is the greatest player there has ever been? The greatest I've ever seen is Johan Cruyff, when he played for New York Cosmos.

Who has been the biggest influence on your career? Rodney Marsh – but not for my footballing ability. He took me on at Tampa Bay Rowdies and helped get me fixed up with Chelsea when I wanted to play in England.

Who has been your toughest opponent? There are so many in the Premiership. The toughest are players with pace and power – like Des Walker and Paul Parker.

If you won a million, what would you buy first? A beach property in West Palm, Florida. I'm not materialistic but it would be nice to have a home overlooking the ocean.

Who is the funniest player you know? QPR's Alan McDonald, who is always cracking jokes. Or my old Rangers team-mate, Kenny Sansom. He does loads of impressions and can keep you entertained all night.

Which team did you support as a boy? Manchester United – because of George Best.

What is the oddest training you've ever done? At Tampa we used to run across golf courses. One day, a couple of players were chased by an alligator who came out of a creek. It's the fastest I've ever seen them run. At the time though it was scary – not funny.

What is your favourite ground? White Hart Lane. I played there in my first game as a Chelsea trialist.

What is your least favourite ground? It used to be my old club Luton, believe or not, because of the artificial surface.

ROY WEGERLE

In the end I grew to like it. But it was terrible for visiting players.

What other sports do you enjoy? I love squash, tennis, golf ... all sports in fact. I was a high-jumper at school and, when I was 15, I once jumped two metres – the third highest in the world for that age group. But soccer took over from athletics.

What dangerous thing would you most like to attempt? Snow skiing.

Who is your favourite sportsman outside football? Sugar Ray Leonard. I'm a big boxing fan and I admired his skill and showmanship. My wife and I used to go to Las Vegas to watch some fights. I once bumped into Marvin Hagler in an hotel... he was enormous!

What's your most prized possession? My Littlewoods Cup loser's medal.

Do you play any musical instruments? No, but I adore music. My wife used to play the guitar.

Who would you most like to meet? Sugar Ray Leonard.

Who is your favourite football manager? Ray Harford, my old boss at Luton. I had a great relationship with him. He got me out of a tough situation at Chelsea where I had hit rock bottom – and got me playing again.

FAVOURITE FILE:

TV programme: *Only Fools And Horses*.

Pop star: Elton John.

Food: Italian.

Drink: I'm teetotal.

Film: 'Sleeping With The Enemy'.

Film star: Richard Gere.

Holiday resort: West Palm Beach in South Florida.

Comedian: Rowan Atkinson.

Single: 'Candle In The Wind' by Elton John.

CD: Elton John's *Madman Across The Water*.

City: New York.

RONNY ROSENTHAL

CAREER RECORD:

Season	Club	Lge App	Lge Goals
1989-90	Luton Town (loan)	–	–
1989-90	Liverpool (loan)	8	7
1990-91	Liverpool	16	5
1991-92	Liverpool	20	3
1992-93	Liverpool	27	6
1993-94	Liverpool	3	0
1993-94	Tottenham	15	2
1994-95	Tottenham	21	0

Appearances

Overseas clubs: Maccabi Haifa, FC Bruges, Standard Liege.
International: Israel (50 apps, 11 goals).

PERSONAL FILE:

Full name: Ronny Rosenthal.

Date of birth: October 4, 1963.

Birthplace: Haifa, Israel.

Brothers and sisters: A brother and two sisters.

Father's job: My dad, Israel, is a jeweller.

Nickname at club: Rocket.

Who was your boyhood hero? Karl-Heinz Rumenigge. I can remember when I was about six years old playing football with my younger brother, Lior, and our friends. Lior went on to become a professional and also played for Israel, in defence and midfield, but a series of injuries forced him to retire.

What has been your biggest thrill in life? Meeting my beautiful wife, Nancy, and having a gorgeous son, Dean.

What has been your biggest disappointment? Not qualifying for the 1990 World Cup Finals with Israel. We lost out to Colombia.

What have been your best and worst moments in soccer? Scoring a hat-trick on my debut for Liverpool and my hat-trick for Spurs against Southampton. The worst was not playing regular first-team football when I was at Anfield.

RONNY ROSENTHAL

Which present-day footballer do you admire most?
Paul Ince, because of his talent, work-rate and versatility.

Who is the greatest player there has ever been? Diego
Maradona – superb skills.

**What has been your greatest sporting achievement
outside football?** At school, I once ran 11.2 secs in the 100
metres.

**What is the strangest thing that's happened to you in a
game?** Once when I was playing for Standard Liege the game
was stopped so the goalie could go to the toilet.

Who do you room with on away trips? Gica Popescu – he
only talks to me in Romanian. I speak five languages – Hebrew,
English, Dutch, French and Romanian.

Who's the best trainer you've seen? My Tottenham team-
mate Darren Anderton. I cannot really say who is the worst.

Which celebrity would make a good football manager?
Rod Stewart, because of his passion for football.

What's the craziest request you've ever had? To be a
guest of honour at a party in South Africa.

**What job would you be doing if you weren't a
footballer?** Stockbroker.

Have you ever needed a kick up the backside? No, I am
self-motivated.

Which team did you support as a boy? Maccabi Haifa – I
joined them at the age of 11. I moved from there to a Belgian
club, FC Bruges, in 1986 and then to Standard Liege before
joining Liverpool.

What TV show would you most like to be in? *Blind Date*,
provided the girls always picked me.

**How would you describe yourself for a lonely hearts
ad?** Goalscorer seeks blonde goalkeeper (female).

What other sports do you enjoy? Waterskiing and
swimming.

**Is there a sporting dream that you would like to have
achieved in another sport?** Winning the U.S. Open tennis
title in New York.

RONNY ROSENTHAL

TV show: *Candid Camera.*
Pop star: Elton John.
Food: Pasta, French cuisine.
Drink: Seven Up, orange juice.
Film: *No Way Out.*
Holiday spot: Monaco.
Comedian: Benny Hill.
Sports star: Lothar Matthaeus.
City: London.
Soap opera: *Baywatch.*
Soap character: Pamela Anderson.

ADRIAN HEATH

Season	Club	Lge App	Lge Goals
1978-79	Stoke City	2	–
1979-80	Stoke City	38	5
1980-81	Stoke City	38	6
1981-82	Stoke City	17	5
1981-82	Everton	22	6
1982-83	Everton	38	10
1983-84	Everton	36	12
1984-85	Everton	17	11
1985-86	Everton	36	10
1986-87	Everton	41	11
1987-88	Everton	29	9
1988-89	Everton	7	2
From Espanol			
1989-90	Aston Villa	9	–
1989-90	Manchester City	12	2
1990-91	Manchester City	35	1
1991-92	Manchester City	28	1
1991-92	Stoke City	6	–
1992-93	Burnley	43	20
1993-94	Burnley	41	9
1994-95	Burnley	27	2

Appearances

International: England U21, England B.

Overseas clubs: Espanol.

PERSONAL FILE:

Full name: Adrian Paul Heath.

Date of birth: January 11, 1961.

Birthplace: Newcastle-under-Lyme.

Father's job: John is a publican.

Brothers and sisters: Two sisters: Claire is a dentist in the Navy, Alexandra is at college.

Nickname: Inchy.

Who was your boyhood hero? As a very young boy, it was George Best. Later, when I was supporting Stoke, it was Alan Hudson.

ADRIAN HEATH

What has been your biggest thrill in life? Playing in my first FA Cup final against Watford in 1984. Everton won 2-0. Graeme Sharp and Andy Gray got our goals.

What has been your biggest disappointment? Getting relegated with Espanol in Spain.

Who would you pick as your greatest player? Every generation has its own but I'd say Diego Maradona because it's harder to play now than it's ever been.

Who has been the greatest influence on your career? My schoolteacher, John Crotty.

Who have been your toughest opponents? Alan Hansen and Mark Lawrenson – the best defensive central partnership ever. They had everything – pace, skill, composure. It used to make me so mad playing against them for Everton in Merseyside derby matches.

What would you be doing if you weren't a footballer? Probably teaching sports at a school or in the forces.

You're 5 ft 7 inches — do you wish you'd been taller? No, you just get on with it. Although I hate it when people say 'a good big 'un will always beat a good little 'un'. I don't think Alan Ball, Billy Bremner and Maradona would agree.

Is your height an advantage? When I was 18 I could still get on a bus for half fare. On the other hand, I kept being asked how old I was in pubs and clubs when I was well over 18!

Has getting the right kit ever been a problem? Only at school, when the shirt used to come through the bottom of my shorts.

What is your funniest moment on a football pitch? Kevin Richardson being chased by a police dog in Germany when I was playing for Everton. He eventually climbed the perimeter fence with this Alsatian going for him. The whole ground was in uproar.

What is the oddest training you've ever done? When I was in Spain, we used to have to do an hour's skipping – not like in a boxing ring but in the school playground. Players would turn the rope and you would have to come in for a couple of jumps and then get out.

ADRIAN HEATH

Who is your favourite sportsman outside of football?
Muhammad Ali, the greatest in and out of the ring.

Who is your favourite football manager? Brian Clough.
Not only is he great to listen to and the most successful, but his
teams played football the way it should be played – unlike the
majority.

Which team did you support as a boy? Stoke.

FAVOURITE FILE:

TV programme: *Only Fools And Horses.*

Pop star: Frank Sinatra and Elvis Presley.

Food: Pasta, paella.

Drink: Spanish red wine, lager.

Films: *Fatal Attraction, My Fair Lady.*

Film stars: Audrey Hepburn, James Cagney, John Wayne.

Holiday spot: Bermuda, where I got married.

Comedian: Bernard Manning.

Single: 'Woman' by John Lennon.

CD: *Frank Sinatra Collection.*

City: Barcelona.

Soap opera: *Coronation Street.*

Francis clashes with goal keeper.

KEVIN FRANCIS

Season	Club	Lge App	Lge Goals
1988-89	Derby Co	–	–
1989-90	Derby Co	8	–
1990-91	Derby Co	2	–
1990-91	Stockport	13	5
1991-92	Stockport	35	15
1992-93	Stockport	42	28
1993-94	Stockport	45	28
1994-95	Stockport	14	10
1994-95	Birmingham	14	7

PERSONAL FILE:

Full name: Kevin Michael Derek Francis.

Date of birth: December 6, 1967.

Birthplace: Moseley.

Father's job: My dad, Raymond, is a lorry driver.

Brothers and sisters: I have three elder sisters. Jackie is a computer consultant, Jaqui is a chef and Arlene is a nurse.

Nickname: Inch Lord, Inches or Inch Man.

What was your childhood ambition? To be successful at my chosen profession and have lots of money. So far, no money.

Who was your boyhood hero? Frank Worthington, the ex-Leicester and England striker. He had so much skill for a big man.

What has been your biggest thrill in life? Playing at Wembley. I played there three times with Stockport. Unfortunately we lost in the Autoglass Trophy final and twice in the play-offs. But I was a winner there at last when Birmingham beat Carlisle in the 1994-95 Auto Windscreens Shield.

What has been your biggest disappointment? Being turned down as a teenager by Birmingham!

Which present-day footballer do you admire most? Former England and West Brom striker Cyrille Regis because of his never-say-die attitude.

KEVIN FRANCIS

Who is the greatest player you have ever seen? Pele. The Brazilian star was a magician with the ball.

Who has been the biggest influence on your career? My father-in-law, because he was always there to support me.

Who would you rate as your toughest opponent? Noel Blake. I played against him three times in a month once and there wasn't enough time for my bumps and bruises to go down.

What would you be doing if you weren't a footballer? A driver or a doorman.

You're 6 ft 7 ins tall. At what age did you top 6 ft? When I turned 16 years of age.

Is your height an advantage? It's handy for jumping queues but the disadvantage is that you're easily spotted.

Has getting the right kit ever been a problem? Although I have size 13 feet I've never had any problems.

What is the oddest training you've ever done? I once spent a week at an Army camp.

Which team did you support as a boy? Birmingham.

What other sports and hobbies do you enjoy? Cycling, weightlifting, driving, eating and sleeping.

Who is your favourite sportsman outside football? Clive Lloyd, the ex-West Indies cricket captain. An all-round gent and great cricketer.

Who are your favourite football managers? Derby's Arthur Cox, for giving me my first chance, Stockport's Danny Bergara for believing in me and Birmingham's Barry Fry, of course.

KEVIN FRANCIS

Pop star: Soul II Soul.

Food: Steak and jacket potatoes.

Drink: Lucozade.

Film: *Boyz 'N' The Hood.*

Animal: Cats.

Holiday resort: St Kitts, West Indies.

TV star: Ted Danson.

Comedian: Harry Enfield.

CD: *Cobra Gold* (reggae).

City: Birmingham.

Soap opera: *Coronation Street.*

A L A N   C O R K

Season	Club	Lge App	Lge Goals
1977-78	Derby Co	–	–
1977-78	Lincoln City (loan)	5	–
1977-78	Wimbledon	17	4
1978-79	Wimbledon	45	22
1979-80	Wimbledon	42	12
1980-81	Wimbledon	41	23
1981-82	Wimbledon	6	–
1982-83	Wimbledon	7	5
1983-84	Wimbledon	42	29
1984-85	Wimbledon	28	11
1985-86	Wimbledon	38	11
1986-87	Wimbledon	30	5
1987-88	Wimbledon	34	9
1988-89	Wimbledon	25	2
1989-90	Wimbledon	31	5
1990-91	Wimbledon	25	5
1991-92	Wimbledon	19	2
1991-92	Sheffield Utd	8	2
1992-93	Sheffield Utd	27	2
1993-94	Sheffield Utd	19	3
1994-95	Fulham	13	3

PERSONAL FILE:

Full name: Alan Graham Cork.

Date of birth: March 4, 1959.

Birthplace: Derby.

Brothers and sisters: One brother, Peter, who works in Coutts Bank in London.

Father's job: My dad, Frank, is a retired process chemist.

Family pets: We have two cats – Cynthia and Albert.

Nickname: Corky.

Who was your boyhood hero? Bobby Charlton. He was one of the first footballers I ever saw on TV and I always wanted to score great goals the way he did.

What has been your biggest thrill in life? Seeing my father's face outside the ground after Wimbledon had beaten

Luton in the 1988 FA Cup semi-final. It's something I will never forget.

What has been your biggest disappointment? When Wimbledon didn't offer me a new contract until they realised I was going.

What has been your worst moment in soccer? When my friend at Wimbledon, Dave Clement, who played for QPR and England, committed suicide.

Which present-day footballer do you admire most? All those over the age of 30 – especially Ray Wilkins.

Who would you pick as your greatest player? Pele. I was brought up on him. I have seen every video and goal – brilliant.

Who have been the greatest influence on your career? My parents at the start for driving me everywhere. Then managers Dario Gradi and Dave Bassett for teaching me all the things I've needed to know over the past 20 years.

Who has been your toughest opponent? Billy Ayre. He used to frighten the life out of me.

What would you be doing if you weren't a footballer? I used to work in the Derbyshire Building Society, so I assume I'd still be there.

What has been your greatest sporting achievement outside football? I fished for Derbyshire when I was younger and I was also involved in the highest third-wicket stand for Derbyshire Boys cricket side.

What is the oddest training you've ever done? At Wimbledon, we had a five-a-side with an invisible ball, and also with a cabbage which was taken from somebody's garden.

Which team did you support as a boy? Derby County.

What other sports do you enjoy? Golf, cricket and horse-racing.

What is your favourite ground? Derby, because it's always special to go back where I started. The atmosphere was great when everybody in the stands used to stamp their feet – a great noise.

Who is your favourite sportsman outside football? Golfer Nick Faldo.

A L A N   C O R K

Who is your favourite football manager? Dave Bassett – he kept giving me contracts.

Do you have any superstitions? I always go out third in line.

What is your most prized possession? My children and my FA Cup winner's medal.

What sporting dream would you like to achieve? I would love to play golf for a living. I would also like to ride a horse in a race at Sandown.

Which world figure do you most admire? Prime Minister John Major. It's an awful job and he tackles it very well under great pressure.

FAVOURITE FILE:

TV programme: *Have I Got News For You.*

Pop star: Morrissey.

Food: Chicken vindaloo.

Drink: Lager.

Film: *The Silence Of The Lambs.*

TV star: John Thaw.

Comedian: Old ones like Tommy Cooper and Eric Morecambe.

CD: *Stars* by Simply Red.

City: Paris.

Soap operas: *Home And Away, Coronation Street.*

Soap character: Alec Gilroy.

BARRY VENISON

Season	Club	Lge App	Lge Goals
1981-82	Sunderland	20	1
1982-83	Sunderland	37	–
1983-84	Sunderland	41	–
1984-85	Sunderland	39	1
1985-86	Sunderland	36	–
1986-87	Liverpool	33	–
1987-88	Liverpool	18	–
1988-89	Liverpool	15	–
1989-90	Liverpool	25	–
1990-91	Liverpool	6	–
1991-92	Liverpool	13	1
1992-93	Newcastle	44	–
1993-94	Newcastle	37	–
1994-95	Newcastle	28	1

Appearances

International: England (1994-) (2 app, 0 goals), England Youth, U21.

PERSONAL FILE:

Full name: Barry Venison.

Date of birth: August 16, 1964.

Birthplace: Consett.

Father's job: My dad David, is a retired miner.

Brothers and sisters: One brother, David.

Family pets: A German Shepherd dog called Jarva.

Nickname: Venners.

Who was your boyhood hero? Johan Cruyff, because of his ability to go past people with his pace and skill.

What has been your biggest thrill in life? Being at the birth of my children – very scary but very rewarding.

What has been your biggest disappointment? My involvement in the Hillsborough disaster when I was with Liverpool. I attended the funerals and memorial services and witnessed the sadness and loss of the bereaved.

What has been your saddest moment in soccer? Losing

BARRY VENISON

1-0 to Norwich in the 1985 Milk Cup Final. I was so honoured to be Sunderland captain but it all ended in tears. The week before Wembley we went to Norwich for a First Division match and won 3-1. But at Wembley we did not perform and Norwich were by far the better team.

What is your best football memory? When I heard I had been called up for England – and making my debut against the U.S.A. My son ordered me to get Alan Shearer's autograph. I wasn't embarrassed about asking another player for his signature. Alan is a daft Geordie like me.

Which present-day footballer do you admire most? John Barnes – who has great strength and skill.

Who would you pick as your greatest player? Pele – he stood above everyone else at the highest level.

Who has been the greatest influence on your career? At school, it was my father. As a pro, Mick Docherty and Alan Durban made me accept responsibility and enjoy it.

Who has been your toughest opponent? Villa's Tony Morley. I had just started playing full-back and he gave me a torrid time.

What would you be doing if you weren't a footballer? Working in the motor trade because of my love for cars.

What is your greatest sporting achievement outside football? Beating Gary Gillespie at tennis every summer.

Have you ever been rejected by a club? Newcastle rejected me as a 14-year-old. I later signed apprentice forms for Sunderland.

What is the oddest training you've ever done? Training on Roker beach. The losers had to go into the freezing cold sea up to their waist.

Which team did you support as a boy? I went through a spell of supporting Leeds before Sunderland.

Which is your favourite ground? Anfield. A superb stadium, a fantastic surface and I have many fond memories of the place. When my contract was up at Sunderland, my wife typed letters and we sent them to every club in what was then the First Division. Luton, Watford, Coventry and Sheffield Wednesday wrote back. Then, right out of the blue, I got a

BARRY VENISON

phone call from Liverpool. There was less than no hesitation about signing.

What sports and hobbies do you enjoy? Tennis and walking my dog.

Is there an unusual food that improves your game? I like fresh fruit salad on the morning of a game.

Who is your favourite sportsman outside football? Nigel Mansell – a brilliant talent and a dedicated sportsman.

Who is your favourite football manager? My Sunderland boss, Alan Durban, although I didn't realise at the time.

Do you have any superstitions? I always put my right shinpad and boot on first.

What are your most prized possessions? My two Championship medals and my FA Cup winner's medal with Liverpool.

Do you ever dream of a particular success in another sport? I would love to drive in a Formula One race.

Which world figure do you most admire? Anyone who gets to the top of their own particular field. It means they have shown the dedication and application to match their ability.

FAVOURITE FILE:

TV programme: *The Bill.*

Pop star: Elvis Presley.

Food: King prawns in garlic.

Drink: Champagne.

Film: *Midnight Express.*

Film star: Patrick Swayze.

Holiday resort: Seychelles.

Comedian: Chubby Brown.

CD: *The Elvis Presley Collection.*

City: Dublin.

Soap opera: *Coronation Street.*

Soap character: Reg Holdsworth.

CRAIG FORREST

Season	Club	Lge App	Lge Goals
1985-86	Ipswich	–	–
1986-87	Ipswich	–	–
1987-88	Ipswich	–	–
1987-88	Colchester (loan)	11	–
1988-89	Ipswich	28	–
1989-90	Ipswich	45	–
1990-91	Ipswich	43	–
1991-92	Ipswich	46	–
1992-93	Ipswich	11	–
1993-94	Ipswich	27	–
1994-95	Ipswich	36	–

Appearances

International: Canada (1988-) (27 apps, 0 goals).

PERSONAL FILE:

Full name: Craig Forrest.

Date of birth: September 20, 1967.

Birthplace: Vancouver, Canada.

Brothers and sisters: I have an elder sister, Lori, who is a legal secretary.

Parents: My dad, Lorne, is a Vancouver fireman. My mum Karron works in a department store.

Nickname: Stax – because I am 6ft 5in. When I first arrived, a team-mate thought I was wearing stacked shoes.

Who was your boyhood hero? Bruce Grobbelaar. Back home in Canada, I watched him play for Vancouver Whitecaps – and I had my picture taken with him when I was 12. We have played against each other several times.

What has been your biggest thrill in life? To play Premier League football.

What has been your biggest disappointment? Missing out on the World Cup in 1994 when Canada failed to qualify.

What has been your best moment in soccer? Playing at the Azteca Stadium in front of 130,000 people – with my mum and dad watching.

CRAIG FORREST

Which present-day footballer do you admire most? My Ipswich team-mate John Wark – because he is now my coach too.

Who would you pick as your greatest player? Pele, for his talent on and off the ball.

What has been your greatest sporting achievement outside football? Finishing first in a club judo competition. I studied judo for five years and reached brown belt status.

Have you ever been rejected by a club? No, Ipswich was my first club. Phil Trenter, a former youth player at Ipswich, moved to Canada and arranged a trial for me here in 1984 when Bobby Ferguson was the boss.

What is the strangest thing that's happened to you in a game? The ball hitting the side-netting and the referee giving a goal.

If you had a tattoo, what would it depict? The Canadian flag and the Union Jack, on my shoulder.

Who do you room with on away trips? Frank Yallop. He always changes the TV channel just when you get interested.

Who have been the greatest influence on your career? My parents have always pushed and supported me when it has been so difficult living away from my family.

Have you ever been mistaken for someone else? John Elway of the Denver Broncos, when I was going through Denver airport.

What is the craziest request you have had from a fan? To autograph her chest.

Have you ever had a kick up the backside in football? Yes, by Ipswich coach Charlie Woods. I think it was because I may have been goofing around.

Which team did you support as a boy? Liverpool.

How would you describe yourself for a lonely hearts ad? Tall, looks like Herman Munster. Hates going out and doesn't like parties. Would anyone be interested?

What other sports do you enjoy? All sports and I love fishing.

CRAIG FORREST

Do you have any superstitions? I put on my right shinguard first.

What are your most prized possessions? The shirts of foreign teams that I have played against.

Do you dream of a particular success in another sport? Playing basketball in the NBA.

FAVOURITE FILE:

TV programme: *Home Improvements, Seinfeld.*
Pop star: Phil Collins.
Drink: Water.
Film: *A Few Good Men.*
Film stars: Beau Bridges, Julia Roberts.
Holiday spots: Mexico, Hawaii.
Sports star: Michael Jordan.
CD: *Tom Petty.*
City: Vancouver.

T O N Y   C O T O N

CAREER RECORD:

Season	Club	Lge App	Lge Goals
1978-79	Birmingham	–	–
1979-80	Birmingham	–	–
1879-80	Hereford (loan)	–	–
1980-81	Birmingham	3	–
1981-82	Birmingham	15	–
1982-83	Birmingham	28	–
1983-84	Birmingham	41	–
1984-85	Birmingham	7	–
1984-85	Watford	33	–
1985-86	Watford	40	–
1986-87	Watford	31	–
1987-88	Watford	37	–
1988-89	Watford	46	–
1989-90	Watford	46	–
1990-91	Manchester City	33	–
1991-92	Manchester City	37	–
1992-93	Manchester City	40	–
1993-94	Manchester City	31	–
1994-95	Manchester City	22	–

Appearances

International: England B.

PERSONAL FILE:

Full name: Anthony Philip Coton.

Date of birth: May 19, 1961.

Birthplace: Tamworth, Staffs.

Father's job: Retired lorry driver.

Home: Four-bed detached house in Cheshire.

Brothers and sisters: My brother Paul is a full-time angler and my sister Carol is a restaurant manager.

Nickname: TC or Colonel Mustard.

What was your childhood ambition? Ever since I was seven, I wanted to be a professional footballer.

Who was your boyhood hero? Goalkeeper Pat Jennings –

121

from the moment I saw him taking crosses one-handed.

What has been your biggest thrill in life? To be at the birth of my two daughters, Natalie and Emily.

What has been your biggest disappointment? Only seeing my daughters every other weekend and on holidays from school. They live with their mother in Hertfordshire.

What has been your saddest moment in soccer? Breaking a thumb a week before an FA Cup semi-final against Tottenham when I was with Watford. I could not play.

Which present-day footballer do you admire most? Neville Southall, the best at our trade.

Who would you pick as your greatest player? Pele.

What is the best part of your job? Getting paid for keeping fit.

What is the worst? Pre-season training and losing.

What would you be doing if you weren't a footballer? Working outdoors, probably on building sites.

If you won a million, what would you buy first? A private plane so I could see my daughters more often.

What is your best quality? I get on easily with people – though they might tell you different.

What is your worst quality? I don't like queuing.

Which team did you support as a boy? Spurs, but I watched Birmingham more – because they were my local side.

Which are your favourite grounds? Anfield and Highbury.

What other sports do you enjoy? Snooker, golf and cricket.

What is your ideal evening out? After a home win, I always go out with my mates from back home for a few pints and usually end up with a curry.

What is the most dangerous thing you've ever done? Changing a wheel on the hard shoulder of the M25.

What dangerous thing would you most like to attempt? To go a round with Mike Tyson.

What is your biggest phobia? I don't have one myself but

T O N Y   C O T O N

I know people who suffer from 'roundaphobia'... a fear of buying a round of drinks.

What is your most prized possession? My TV remote control.

Who would you most like to meet? Princess Di.

What will you do when you stop playing? I hope to stay in the game coaching.

What was the most embarrassing moment of your life? When I was at school, I asked a girl out for the first time and she said no. I never bother asking anyone now.

Which world figure do you admire most? Stormin' Norman Schwarzkopf, for the way he led the Iraq conflict.

FAVOURITE FILE:

TV programme: *Only Fools And Horses.*
Pop stars: Elton John, Phil Collins.
Food: Indian, egg and chips.
Drink: Tea, lager top.
Film: *Planes, Trains and Automobiles.*
Film star: John Candy.
Resort: Florida.
TV star: David Jason.
Comedian: Chubby Brown.
Single: 'You To Me Are Everthing' by the Real Thing.
CD: *Singles* by Squeeze.
Soap: Coronation Street.
Soap character: Reg Holdsworth.

Spencer powers in on goal.

JOHN SPENCER

Season	Club	Lge App	Lge Goals
1986-87	Glasgow Rangers	–	–
1987-88	Glasgow Rangers	–	–
1988-89	Glasgow Rangers	–	–
1988-89	Morton (loan)	4	1
To Lisbung, Hong Kong (loan)			
1990-91	Glasgow Rangers	5	1
1991-92	Glasgow Rangers	8	1
1992-93	Chelsea	23	7
1993-94	Chelsea	19	5
1994-95	Chelsea	29	11

Appearances

International: Scotland (1994-) (4 apps, 0 goals), U21.
Overseas clubs: Lisboung, HK.

PERSONAL FILE:

Full name: John Spencer.

Date of birth: September 11, 1970.

Birthplace: Glasgow.

Home: Hertfordshire.

Brothers and sisters: A younger brother, Tony, who works in a Glasgow bar.

Mother's job: My mum Christine works in a bookies' shop.

Family pets: A Rottweiler called Sasha.

Nickname: Spenno.

Who was your boyhood hero? Kenny Dalglish. He was the best thing ever to come out of Scotland. He is a legend.

What has been your biggest thrill in life? Being at the birth of my little girl, Chantelle.

What has been your biggest disappointment in life? Not playing more for Glasgow Rangers and losing the 1994 FA Cup Final when Chelsea were beaten by Manchester United.

What has been your saddest moment in soccer? Leaving Rangers. My boss there Graeme Souness sent me for a spell in Hong Kong. He knew it was a make-or-break time for

JOHN SPENCER

me. I had matured as much as I could in the reserves but I was still not anywhere near the first team. He told me I would learn the kind of things which I couldn't learn in the reserves at Ibrox. He was right and I'll always be grateful to him and to Walter Smith. These guys have helped my career more than any others.

Which present-day footballers do you admire most?
Ally McCoist and Mark Hateley. They continue to score goals at the very top level, season after season.

Who would you pick as your greatest player? Diego Maradona. He won the World Cup almost single-handedly, and had everything you need to succeed.

Who has been the greatest influence on your career?
In my younger days, it was John Kerr who took me to Rangers. Now it is my father-in-law, Bill Davies, who gives me loads of advice.

What has been your greatest sporting achievement outside football? When I beat my father-in-law 5-1 at snooker. He went home to his wife and said that he wasn't going to play me again. He reckoned I was always talking when he was taking his shots. I wasn't, honestly.

Have you ever been rejected by a club? I had trials at a few clubs, including Newcastle, but I only wanted to sign for Rangers. Celtic invited me for a trial but the letter arrived on the day I was going off on a holiday to Spain. I wrote back saying I would be in touch when I returned but I never got around to it.

What is the oddest training you've ever done? Our old Chelsea boss Dave Webb had us slide-tackling footballs. There were two footballs 15 yards apart and we had to run, jump and slide-tackle them. It was so funny – but nobody laughed to his face.

Which team did you support as a boy? Liverpool.

Which is your favourite ground? Ibrox and Old Trafford. The two best stadiums in Britain for the two best clubs.

Which is your least favourite ground? Oldham.

What other sports and hobbies do you enjoy? I am a boxing fanatic. I also like sitting on the sofa because I am too lazy to do anything else.

JOHN SPENCER

Is there an unusual food that improves your game?
Bananas and plenty of Evian mineral water.

Who is your favourite sportsman outside football?
I have three – boxers Chris Eubank and Mike Tyson, plus
basketball star Michael Jordan.

Do you dream of a particular success in another sport?
Winning the Wimbledon men's singles title.

Which world figure do you most admire? Michael Jordan.

You're 5 ft 5 in – has that been a problem? No. God put
grass on the ground and that's where I feel the ball should be
played.

**What do you recall of your Cup Winners' Cup quarter-
final goal for Chelsea against FK Austria when you ran
70 yards to score?** I kept thinking they had a player lying in
the grass who was going to jump up and tackle me.

FAVOURITE FILE:

TV programme: *NYPD Blue*.

Pop star: Snoop Doggy Dog, Dr Dre.

Food: Pasta.

Drink: Evian mineral water.

Film: *Godfather 3*.

Film stars: Robert De Niro, Demi Moore.

Holiday resort: Pollok, Glasgow.

CD: *The Chronic* by Dr Dre.

Bright (left) with former Palace team mate, Ian Wright.

MARK BRIGHT

Season	Club	Lge App	Lge Goals
1981-82	Port Vale	2	–
1982-83	Port Vale	1	1
1983-84	Port Vale	26	9
1984-85	Leicester City	16	–
1985-86	Leicester City	24	6
1986-87	Leicester City	2	0
1986-87	Crystal Palace	28	8
1987-88	Crystal Palace	38	25
1988-89	Cystal Palace	46	20
1989-90	Crystal Palace	36	12
1990-91	Crystal Palace	32	9
1991-92	Crystal Palace	42	17
1992-93	Crystal Palace	5	1
1992-93	Sheffield Wed	30	11
1993-94	Sheffield Wed	40	19
1994-95	Sheffield Wed	37	11

PERSONAL FILE:

Full name: Mark Abraham Bright.

Date of birth: June 6, 1962.

Birthplace: Stoke-on-Trent.

Brothers and sisters: One brother, Phil, and three sisters – Marie, Sharon and Maureen.

Family pets: None, I don't like pets.

Nickname: Brighty.

What was your childhood ambition? To be famous.

Who was your boyhood hero? Most players say Pele because, when we were young, we all wanted to be him.

What has been your biggest thrill in life? Playing in the FA Cup Final for Crystal Palace against Manchester United. And playing for Sheffield Wednesday in the FA Cup and Coca-Cola Cup Finals against Arsenal.

What have been your biggest disappointments? Losing those games.

What has been your saddest moment? Wasting a season

with Crystal Palace. John Salako received a terrible injury and we achieved nothing at all.

Which present-day footballer do you admire most?
Gary Lineker. He produced the goods at every level while maintaining a modest approach and level head. A great ambassador for the country. He taught me a lot – especially temperament. When you saw him getting kicked and thumped by the best defenders in the world and just get up with only a shake of his head it made you realise what a great player he was.

Who would you pick as your greatest players? Pele and Maradona – both footballing geniuses with the ability to produce the unbelievable.

Who have been the greatest influence on your career?
Port Vale manager John Rudge and Villa youth coach Dave Richardson. Both helped me in the early years and I have now reaped the benefit. I'd work until 2.30 pm and then get the bus to Port Vale where I'd been taken on part-time. John Rudge, who was the coach then, would wait behind to help me. I owe him a lot for that.

Who has been your toughest opponent? Roy McFarland, when he was playing for Bradford City against Port Vale. He was too experienced for me at the time.

What would you be doing if you weren't a footballer?
I'm a qualified hydraulic engineer and went to college for five years on day release, so I suppose I would be doing that. I was earning £120 a week and took a drop to join Port Vale. My boss at work Bill Thompson said you had to take chances in life. I just believed I would be a success.

What has been your greatest sporting achievement outside football? Playing golf, I was once six inches away from a hole-in-one.

What is your funniest moment on the pitch? Andy Gray once trained in a sheepskin coat because there were no sweat tops. After that, he was nicknamed Larry The Lamb.

Which team did you support as a boy? Chelsea, because everyone was supporting Stoke in the 1972 League Cup.

Which is your favourite ground? Anfield – a big stage and atmosphere.

MARK BRIGHT

What other sports and hobbies do you enjoy? Tennis, a bit of golf, reading and boxing.

Is there an unusual food that improves your game? I don't know if it helps but I always eat pasta on Thursdays and Fridays because of its slow-burn carbohydrates.

Who is your favourite sportsman? Michael Jordan – a mega star in the true sense.

Who is your favourite football manager? John McGrath – you always have a fondness for your first manager (well, some players do!). And you have to respect Mr Clough for his achievements.

Can you recall first meeting Ian Wright at Palace? We hit it off immediately, started to room together on away trips, became partners on the pitch and friends off it and our friendship has grown. Ian's mum looked after me when I first came down to London. We used to eat Jamaican food at her house. You need help and stability when you first come to a big city – and Ian's family gave me that.

FAVOURITE FILE:

TV programme: Most sports shows.

Pop stars: Michael Jackson, Prince, Madonna.

Food: Pasta or Thai.

Drink: Soft drinks or white wine.

Film: *Goodfellas*.

Film stars: Robert De Niro, Warren Beatty, Meryl Streep.

Holiday resort: Caribbean.

TV star: David Jason.

Comedian: Eddie Murphy.

CD: *Off The Wall* by Michael Jackson.

Book: *Empire of Deceit* by Dean Allison and Bruce B. Henderson.

RICK HOLDEN

CAREER RECORD:

Season	Club	Lge App	Lge Goals
1985-86	Burnley	1	0
1986-87	Halifax	32	2
1987-88	Halifax	35	10
1987-88	Watford	10	2
1988-89	Watford	32	6
1989-90	Oldham	45	9
1990-91	Oldham	42	5
1991-92	Oldham	42	5
1992-93	Manchester City	41	3
1993-94	Manchester City	9	–
1993-94	Oldham	29	6
1994-95	Oldham	28	3

PERSONAL FILE:

Full name: Richard William Holden.

Date of birth: September 9, 1964.

Birthplace: Skipton, North Yorkshire.

Cars: An E-reg XR3i – I bought it at Watford, it's a bit knackered but does a job – and a Volvo Estate for all the family.

Brothers and sisters: A younger sister, Jennifer. She is in the building trade but is currently distracted by her children, Michael and Isobel.

Father's job: Roger, now retired, worked in teaching/industry.

Family pets: Three cats – Minging, Dougal and Mutley.

Nickname: Wur or Scratcher.

Who was your boyhood hero? Mario Kempes – long hair, great skill, socks around his ankles. Good job for him he was Argentinian and not English because they wouldn't have played him here.

What has been your biggest thrill in life? Although it sounds corny, it was my wedding day.

What has been your biggest disappointment? At one stage I had so many that it was depressing. But at 19 I changed totally and now nothing disappoints me to the degree that it is life-affecting. Life is for living, so get on with it and don't let things get you down.

What have been your best and worst moments in soccer? The best was helping Oldham win the Second Division championship on the last day of the season. The worst was falling out with Steve Harrison at Watford in 1988. Luckily it worked out when I signed for Oldham in 1989.

Who would you pick as your greatest player? Diego Maradona – greatest talent ever who could make the ball talk. He has been victimised and hated by people who would have loved him if he had been English.

What has been your greatest sporting achievement outside football? Winning the Craven Cup with Skipton L.M.S. in 1984 and the Cricket Wynn Cup with Embsay in 1992.

Have you ever been rejected by a club? I wrote to Aldershot when I was 17 as they were the first club in the directory. I received a polite 'No thanks'. Other than that, Burnley showed me the door.

What is the strangest thing that's happened to you in a game? Getting sent off against Arsenal on my second home debut for Oldham.

Who do you room with on away trips? Jon Hallworth, a great friend and a loyal subject. However, his phone obsession drives me to swearing at his constant incoming phone calls.

Who has been the greatest influence on your career? My dad, for not pressuring me into anything; and Billy Ayre at Halifax taught me a thing or two.

Who is the best trainer you have seen? Neil Redfearn, the fittest man I have ever seen, who was treated badly at Oldham.

Which celebrity would make a good football manager? Possibly Cilla Black – 'win lads and I won't sing'.

What is the craziest request you have received from a fan? I once signed a fan's forehead during Oldham's hey-day.

Have you ever needed a kick up the backside in football? No. Joe Royle thought I needed it several times but in truth, Joe, a rest and an explanation would have been better.

RICK HOLDEN

Which teams did you support as a boy? Leeds and Embsay Rovers.

What rock group would you most like to be in? Deep Purple and to be Ritchie Blackmore.

What other sports do you enjoy? Cricket and golf.

Do you have any superstitutions? No, we in football prefer to call them routines.

What is your most prized possession? My health. I can't say the wife as she is not a possession.

Do you dream of a particular success in another sport? To win an Ashes series in Australia as captain and shove it where the sun doesn't shine. They call us whingeing Poms but nobody can match the Aussies for being bad losers.

FAVOURITE FILE:

TV programme: *Blackadder*.

Pop star: Ritchie Blackmore.

Food: Fish, chips and mushy peas; chicken spinach madras at the Aagrah in Skipton.

Drink: Taylor's Landlord bitter.

Film: *Outlaw Josey Wales*.

Film star: Clint Eastwood.

TV star: Eric Morecambe – died too young.

Comedians: Laurel and Hardy.

CD: *Rainbow Rising*, by Rainbow.

Cities: Leeds, Buenos Aires.

MARK HUGHES

CAREER RECORD:

Season	Club	Lge App	Lge Goals
1980-81	Manchester United	–	–
1981-82	Manchester United	–	–
1982-83	Manchester United	–	–
1983-84	Manchester United	11	4
1984-85	Manchester United	38	16
1985-86	Manchester United	40	17
1988-89	Manchester United	38	14
1989-90	Manchester United	37	13
1990-91	Manchester United	31	10
1991-92	Manchester United	39	11
1992-93	Manchester United	41	15
1993-94	Manchester United	36	11
1994-95	Manchester United	34	8

Appearances

International: Wales (1984-) (56 apps, 12 goals), Youth, U21.
Overseas clubs: 1986-88: Barcelona, Bayenn Munich (loan).

PERSONAL FILE:

Full name: Leslie Mark Hughes.

Date of birth: November 1, 1963.

Birthplace: Wrexham.

Home: Cheshire.

Brothers and sisters: One sister, Jackie, who is a housewife.

Nickname: Sparky.

What was your childhood ambition? To play for my country at all levels – an ambition I have achieved.

Who was your boyhood hero? Wrexham team (Mickey Thomas, Bobby Shinton etc) of the late seventies.

What has been your biggest thrill in football? There have been so many recently – winning the title at last for United after so many years, the Double, and the European Cup Winners' Cup triumph in Rotterdam.

What has been your biggest disappointment? The failure of Wales to qualify for a major championship. Every player wants to play in the world's biggest tournaments.

MARK HUGHES

What has been your saddest moment in soccer?
Missing out on Mexico '86 when Wales were held 1-1 by
Scotland after that controversial penalty.

Which present-day footballer do you admire most? My
old Manchester United team-mate Bryan Robson, because of his
desire to win and his leadership.

Who would you pick as your greatest player? My vote
would go to George Best. He had the lot.

What is the best part of your job? Scoring and winning.

What is the worst part? Playing at Christmas. It's tough
being away from the family at that time.

What would you be doing if you weren't a footballer?
I haven't a clue.

If you won a million, what would you do first? Get some
golf lessons from Ian Woosnam.

What is your best quality? I have a lot of patience with the
kids.

What is your worst quality? My wife, Jill, says I'm very
untidy.

Which team did you support as a boy? I followed two
teams – Wrexham and Chelsea.

Apart from your home ground, what's your favourite?
Cardiff Arms Park because of the atmosphere and impact it has
on Welsh football.

What is your least favourite? Norwich's Carrow Road. It's
too far away and I went a long time without winning there.

What other sports do you enjoy? A round of golf when
I have some spare time.

What is your ideal evening out? A meal with my wife and
friends.

What is the most dangerous thing you have done?
I once dived into the children's end of a swimming pool and split
my head open.

What dangerous thing would you most like to attempt?
I would love to have a crack at driving a Grand Prix car.

MARK HUGHES

What is your biggest phobia? Anything with wings – birds, planes, anything.

Do you have any superstitions? I always put on my left boot first.

What are your most prized possessions? My PFA Footballer of the Year awards – and the medals I have picked up with United in the last few years.

Do you play any musical instruments? No, but I used to learn the violin at school.

Who would you most like to meet? Princess Diana.

What will you do after you stop playing? Something in the property development line.

Which world figure do you most admire? Mikhail Gorbachev, for the way he has helped the people of Russia.

FAVOURITE FILE:

TV programme: *Open All Hours*.
Pop stars: Robert Palmer and U2.
Food: Poached salmon.
Drink: Milk.
Film: *Flatliners*.
Film star: Julia Roberts.
Animal: Labrador dog.
Holiday resort: Sardinia.
TV star: David Jason.
Comedian: Rowan Atkinson.
Single: 'Bad' by U2.
CD: *Unforgettable Fire* by U2.
City: Barcelona.
Soap opera: *Coronation Street*.
Soap character: Jack Duckworth.

B R Y A N R O Y

Season	Club	Lge App	Lge Goals
1994-95	Nottingham Forest	37	11

Appearances

International: Holland (1990-) (32 apps, 9 goals).
Overseas clubs: Ajax, Foggia.

PERSONAL FILE:

Full name: Bryan Edward Steven Roy.

Date of birth: February 12, 1970.

Birthplace: Amsterdam.

Home: I have a cottage.

Cars: A BMW 316i, a BMW 325i convertible and a Range Rover.

Brothers and sisters: A sister who is a student.

Father's job: My dad is an accountant.

Nickname: Dutch.

Who was your boyhood hero? That would be Argentinian star Diego Maradona.

What has been your biggest thrill in life? The birth of my daughter, Jamy Lee, and getting married.

What has been your worst moment in soccer? Leaving Ajax. I had some tactical problems when Louis van Gaal took over as coach. I like to play intuitively but van Gaal wanted me to play under a strict system. I did not think that was helping my football development.

Which present-day footballer do you admire most? My Holland team-mate, Marco Van Basten.

Who would you pick as your greatest player? Diego Maradona. He was blessed with great skills and great vision, and his achievements show he is the greatest.

What has been your greatest sporting achievement outside football? Winning the UEFA Cup in 1992 when Ajax beat Torino on away goals after the games ended 2-2 on aggregate.

BRYAN ROY

Who do you room with on away trips? David Phillips. He doesn't annoy me at all!

Who has been the greatest influence on your career? Johan Cruyff. He gave me my first-team chance at Ajax when I was 17 and has always believed in me. I owe him a lot. He gave me self-confidence and that, to me, is the most important thing for a footballer. Then he can give of his best.

How did you cope in the first team at 17? I was hailed as one of the new heroes of the country. People expected me to behave like a grown-up but I was only a boy. I was treated a lot differently than Ryan Giggs. Manchester United have protected him really well. When I hit the headlines there was nobody to help me out. A lot of people wrote me off but a select few kept faith in me.

Who is the best trainer you have seen? Johan Cruyff again. His records as a player and a coach say it all. He taught me a lot of important things – positioning, being tactically aware and lots of other things.

How different is playing in the Premiership to playing elsewhere in Europe? Clubs play a lot more games in the season and I have found that tough from a physical point of view.

Which team did you support as a boy? Ajax.

How would you describe yourself for a lonely hearts ad? Relaxed.

What other sports do you enjoy? Tennis.

What are your most prized possessions? My wife and daughter.

B R Y A N   R O Y

TV programme: *The Oprah Winfrey Show.*
Pop star: Luther Vandross.
Food: Indonesian.
Drink: Red wine.
Film: *Pulp Fiction.*
Film star: Richard Gere.
Holiday spot: French Riviera.
Comedian: Eddie Murphy.
CD: *Black Street.*
Cities: London, Rome.
Soap opera: *Fresh Prince Of Bel Air.*
Soap character: Will Smith.

SCOTT SELLARS

CAREER RECORD:

Season	Club	Lge App	Lge Goals
1982-83	Leeds	1	–
1983-84	Leeds	19	3
1984-85	Leeds	39	7
1985-86	Leeds	17	2
1986-87	Blackburn	32	4
1987-88	Blackburn	42	7
1988-89	Blackburn	46	2
1989-90	Blackburn	43	14
1990-91	Blackburn	9	1
1991-92	Blackburn	30	7
1992-93	Leeds	7	–
1992-93	Newcastle	13	2
1993-94	Newcastle	30	3
1994-95	Newcastle	19	1

Appearances

International: England U21.

PERSONAL FILE:

Full name: Scott Sellars.

Date of birth: November 27, 1965.

Birthplace: Sheffield.

Brothers and sisters: A younger brother, Christopher, who is an accountant.

Father's job: My dad is a panel beater.

Family pets: A cat called Chloe.

Nickname: Scoot – I don't know why.

What have been your best and worst moments in soccer? Winning promotion with Newcastle and Blackburn. The worst were losing three successive play-offs with Blackburn. My final game for Rovers was the last of the season when we beat Leicester in the play-off final to make the Premiership. Having gone so close three times before, there was nobody happier than me when Rovers finally went up. I had come to the end of my contract and wanted a longer deal than the one I was offered. So I turned it down and Leeds came in. Even so, I was really sad to leave.

145

SCOTT SELLARS

Were you surprised when Newcastle bought you?
It came out of the blue. Newcastle were 13 points clear at the
top of the First Division and hardly looked as if they needed my
help. I sat down with Kevin Keegan and my mind went back to
one of my first games with Leeds as an 18-year-old against
Newcastle at St James' Park, the year the gaffer took them back
up to the First Division as a player. Now here he was telling me
I was a player he had always admired. *He* had always admired
me! I couldn't believe my ears. I signed immediately and made
my debut the next day.

Which present-day footballer do you admire most?
Gordon Strachan. I have played alongside him and against him.
His talent, workrate and dedication are tremendous.

**What has been your greatest sporting achievement
outside football?** When I was at school I sparred with
middleweight boxing champion Herol 'Bomber' Graham. I could
not get near him!

Have you ever been rejected by a club? Happily no, but
I was only 5ft 3in at 15. I was always the titch who sat on the
bench. Then I put on a few inches and made it to Leeds. Sadly
the game was becoming more of a physical contest. One day
Billy Bremner sat me down and said he felt I was too small to
survive.

What is the strangest thing that has happened to you?
I fell over when I was warming up as a substitute.

Who do you room with on away trips? Ruel Fox. He's
always on the mobile phone to his mate, Chris Sutton.

Who has been the greatest influence on your career?
My father helped me enormously when I was young. When
I became a professional I got a lot of help from Eddie Gray, my
first manager at Leeds.

**Who is the best trainer you have seen — and the
worst?** Barry Venison always gives 100 per cent. The worst?
Well, the manager is having a bad spell in the five-a-sides. It has
lasted two years.

Which celebrity would make a good football manager?
Reg Holdsworth. He showed good managerial qualities at
Bettabuys.

SCOTT SELLARS

Have you ever needed a kick up the backside in football? Don Mackay at Blackburn told me to be more emotional on the pitch. He said I was too laid-back.

Which team did you support as a boy? Sheffield Wednesday.

How would you describe yourself for a lonely hearts ad? Skinny, bow-legged old man who can't get a bird.

What irritates you most in football? Old players who have a go at present players. I hate negative tactics – football should be exciting to watch.

Do you have any superstitions? I always put my shorts on last.

Do you dream of a particular success in another sport? To win The Open golf tournament.

FAVOURITE FILE:

TV programme: *Cheers.*

Pop star: Prince, INXS.

Food: Anything unhealthy – bacon and eggs, fish and chips.

Film: *Tombstone.*

Film star: Robin Williams.

Holiday spot: America.

Sports star: John Daly.

CD: *Kick* by INXS.

City: Newcastle.

Soap opera: *Coronation Street.*

Soap character: Reg Holdsworth.

JOHN McGINLAY

Season	Club	Lge App	Lge Goals
1988-89	Shrewsbury	16	5
1989-90	Shrewsbury	44	22
1990-91	Bury	25	9
1990-91	Millwall	2	–
1991-92	Millwall	25	8
1992-93	Millwall	7	2
1992-93	Bolton	34	16
1993-94	Bolton	39	25
1994-95	Bolton	37	16
	Play-offs	3	2

Appearances

International: Scotland (1994-) (7 apps, 2 goals).

PERSONAL FILE:

Full name: John McGinlay.

Date of birth: April 8, 1964.

Birthplace: Inverness.

Brothers and sisters: Two younger brothers-David, who plays part-time for Huntly in the Highland League, and Alistair, who works for a saw mill and plays for Fort William in the Highland League.

Father's job: Arthur is a quarry machine operator.

Family pets: A Lhasa Apso dog called Ben.

Nickname: McGin.

Who was your boyhood hero? Denis Law or Jimmy Johnstone – two fantastic players. Later on it was my idol Kenny Dalglish.

What has been your biggest thrill in life? The birth of my boys and scoring a goal in our FA Cup win at Liverpool in January 1993. More recently it has been the Coca-Cola Cup Final against Liverpool and winning the 1995 play-offs against Reading to reach the Premiership.

What has been your biggest disappointment in life? Not making the grade at an earlier age.

149

JOHN McGINLAY

What has been your saddest moment in soccer? The death of Jock Stein at the Scotland-Wales game. Personally, it was being knocked out of the FA Cup by non-League Chorley when I was at Bury. They beat us 2-1. Then there was the Coca-Cola Cup defeat by Liverpool.

Which present-day footballer do you admire most? Sheffield Wednesday's David Hirst. He is a fantastic striker, a scorer of great goals – he should be playing for England.

Who would you pick as your greatest player? George Best – a genius.

What has been your greatest sporting achievement outside football? Coming equal first with Colin Cooper on a Millwall FC golf day.

Have you ever been rejected by a club? I had a month's trial with Sunderland when I was 21 and playing for Nairn County. The weather was bad and I only played two games. I did all right but they thought I was too old.

What is the strangest thing that's happened in a game? Victor Kasule scored for Shrewsbury and tried to do a Hugo Sanchez somersault. He broke a toe and was out for six weeks.

Who has been the greatest influence on your career? Ian McNeil, who signed me for Shrewsbury when I was 24. He gave me my big chance and I will always be grateful to him.

What is the oddest of training you've ever done? Running up hills at Church Stretton when I was at Shrewsbury. They were so steep that even the sheep could not get to the top.

What would you be doing if you weren't a footballer? I had various jobs on building sites when I was a part-timer – and I've done other odd jobs. I hated them all.

Which team did you support as a boy? Celtic.

Which is your favourite ground? Anfield – I will always remember the night Bolton beat Liverpool.

What other sports do you enjoy? Golf.

Is there a special food that improves your game? I always eat steak the night before and porridge for breakfast.

JOHN McGINLAY

Who is your favourite sportsman outside football? Nick Faldo – simply the best.

Who are your favourite football managers? Brian Clough – a great character who is not afraid to admit his mistakes – and Bruce Rioch – my former manager at Bolton. He has signed me twice now – a hard but fair man.

FAVOURITE FILE:

TV programmes: *Only Fools And Horses, One Foot In The Grave.*

Pop stars: Phil Collins, Rod Stewart, Cher.

Food: Steak, lamb chops.

Drink: Lager.

Film: *Ghost.*

Film stars: John Wayne, James Cagney, Julia Roberts.

Holiday spot: Majorca.

TV star: Jimmy Nail.

Comedian: Freddie Starr.

CD: Meatloaf's *Bat Out Of Hell.*

City: Glasgow.

Soap opera: *Coronation Street.*

Soap character: Reg Holdsworth.

PAUL McGRATH

Season	Club	Lge App	Lge Goals
1981-82	Manchester United	–	–
1982-83	Manchester United	14	3
1983-84	Manchester United	9	1
1984-85	Manchester United	23	–
1985-86	Manchester United	40	3
1986-87	Manchester United	35	2
1987-88	Manchester United	22	2
1988-89	Manchester United	20	1
1989-90	Aston Villa	35	1
1990-91	Aston Villa	35	–
1991-92	Aston Villa	41	1
1992-93	Aston Villa	42	4
1993-94	Aston Villa	30	1
1994-95	Aston Villa	30	–

Appearances
International: Rep of Ireland (1985-) (74 apps, 7 goals).

PERSONAL FILE:

Full name: Paul McGrath.

Date of birth: December 4, 1959.

Birthplace: Ealing, London.

Family: Married to Caroline. I have with three children: Christopher, Mitchell and Jordan.

Brothers and sisters: My sister, Okune, died in 1993. I have a niece, Maiwa.

Family pets: Cat and a hamster.

Nickname: Macca is the only one printable.

Who were your boyhood heroes? The Chelsea trio of Ian Hutchinson, Alan Hudson and Charlie Cooke.

What has been your biggest thrill in life? The births of my sons.

What have been your best and worst moments in soccer? Playing in the World Cup quarter-finals for the Republic against Italy in Rome in 1990. The worst moment was 90 minutes later when we had lost 1-0.

153

PAUL McGRATH

Which present-day footballer do you admire most?
Italy's Franco Baresi.

Who would you pick as your greatest player? Pele – he
was a pure genius.

**What has been your greatest sporting achievement
outside football?** Sprinting at school in Dublin.

**What is the strangest thing that's happened to you in a
game?** I fell flat on my back playing for Aston Villa against
Swindon and became disorientated. I jumped up and started to
attack the wrong end.

Who do you room with on away trips? At Aston Villa it
used to be Earl Barrett. Being younger, he should have done as
he was told and made me a coffee when I asked him.

Who has been the greatest influence on your career?
Bryan Whitehouse. He took a lot of rough edges off me when
I first went to Manchester United. I was 22 and playing for St
Patrick's Athletic in the Irish League when United came in for
me. I was spotted by Billy Behan, United's scout in Ireland.

**Who is the best trainer you have seen — and the
worst?** The best was my Manchester United team-mate Bryan
Robson. Even after a night out, he could outrun anybody at the
club. The worst is myself. After a night out, I can't move.

Have you ever been mistaken for someone else? I've
been called Fred West by my Republic team-mate Tony Cascarino.

**Have you ever needed a kick up the backside in
football?** My backside is in bits. It has been kicked by Ron
Atkinson, Graham Taylor, Jack Charlton, Alex Ferguson, Alex
Ferguson, Alex Ferguson...

Which team did you support as a boy? Chelsea.

What rock group would you most like to be in? Kenny
G. I'd love to be able to play an instrument that well.

What hobbies do you enjoy? Sleeping and playing brag.

Who or what irritates you most in football? Players who
deliberately go out to hurt other players. Fortunately, there
aren't too many of them about.

What are your most prized possessions? My boys and
Caroline.

PAUL McGRATH

Do you dream of a particular success in another sport?
I'd love to have been a top sprinter.

FAVOURITE FILE:

TV programme: *Absolutely Fabulous.*
Pop stars: Chicago, Kenny G.
Food: Caroline's roast dinner.
Drink: Lager, Diet Coke.
Film star: Michelle Pfeiffer.
Holiday spot: Mauritius.
TV star: Joanna Lumley.
Comedian: Chubby Brown.
City: Dublin.

MARK ROBINS

CAREER RECORD:

Season	Club	Lge App	Lge Goals
1986-87	Manchester United	–	–
1987-88	Manchester United	–	–
1988-89	Manchester United	10	–
1989-90	Manchester United	17	7
1990-91	Manchester United	19	4
1991-92	Manchester United	2	–
1992-93	Norwich City	37	15
1993-94	Norwich City	13	1
1994-95	Norwich City	17	4
1994-95	Leicester	17	5

Appearances

International: England U21.

PERSONAL FILE:

Full name: Mark Gordon Robins.

Date of birth: December 22, 1969.

Birthplace: Ashton-Under-Lyme.

Brothers and sisters: A younger brother Gareth, who is looking to join the Army, and a younger sister Lisa, who is an interior designer.

Parents: My dad Gordon is a retired policeman. My mum Marilyn is a midwife.

Pets: We have a labrador called Bouncer and a beagle named Sam.

Nickname: Robbo.

What have been your biggest thrills in life? The birth of my daughter, Georgia – and playing professional football.

What have been your biggest disappointments? Not getting a regular place at Manchester United. I was disappointed my move to Norwich didn't work out. I enjoyed a good first season there and am looking forward to my time with Leicester.

What have been your best and worst moments in soccer? The best was winning the FA Cup with Manchester United. The worst was when I injured a cartilage against Bayern Munich – which meant I missed Norwich's good run in the UEFA Cup. In all, I was out five months.

MARK ROBINS

Which present-day footballer do you admire most?
Alan Shearer. He came back from a nasty ligament injury as if he
had never been away.

Who would you pick as your greatest player? There are
a lot of great players still playing. It is difficult to say who is the
best because we are in a different era from Pele, George Best
etc. Today I admire people like Hagi, Matthaeus and Voller.

Have you ever been rejected by a club? No, the clubs
I attended all wanted to sign me. I went to most of the
Lancashire clubs – Manchester City, Blackburn, Burnley and
Manchester United. As soon as I went to United I wanted to
sign. Ron Atkinson was the manager at the time and,
fortunately, they wanted me.

**What is the strangest thing that's happened to you in a
game?** That was when a female streaker ran across the pitch
during a game. For some reason, I can't seem to remember
what match it was.

Who do you room with on away trips? At Norwich
I roomed with Gary Megson. He has a lucky mascot – an old,
horrible bag made of rabbit skin which he takes everywhere.

Who has been the greatest influence on your career?
My dad. He has taken time out with me since I was 10 years old
to help keep my fitness up during the summer. I played for his
team in Oldham called Boundary Park Juniors. He's still involved
with them. On top of that, he has helped me overcome any
disappointments in my career.

Have you ever been mistaken for someone else? Yes,
I was in a shop once and someone thought I was the shop
assistant.

Which celebrity would make a good football manager?
I don't know but the bloke who played the Barcelona manager in
the TV show *All In The Game* definitely would not!

Which team did you support as a boy? At first, I was a
Junior Blue with Manchester City. But I converted to
Manchester United when I was eight years old. There was a
good atmosphere at the ground and they played attractive,
attacking football.

What TV show would you most like to be in? *Baywatch*.

MARK ROBINS

What other sports and hobbies do you enjoy? Golf and days out with the family.

What are your most prized possessions? The medals I won during my time with Manchester United – the FA Cup, European Cup Winners Cup and Charity Shield.

FAVOURITE FILE:

Food: Indian.

Drink: Blackcurrant and soda.

Film: *Rising Sun*.

Film stars: Sean Connery, Robert De Niro.

Holiday spot: Cyprus.

Comedian: Gary Megson.

Sports star: Daley Thompson.

CD: *Miaow* by The Beautiful South.

Cities: Manchester, Norwich.

Soap opera: *Coronation Street*.

Soap character: Jack Duckworth.

TEDDY SHERINGHAM

Season	Club	Lge App	Lge Goals
1983-84	Millwall	7	1
1984-85	Millwall	–	–
1984-85	Aldershot (loan)	5	1
1985-86	Millwall	18	4
1986-87	Millwall	42	13
1987-88	Millwall	43	22
1988-89	Millwall	33	11
1989-90	Millwall	31	9
1990-91	Millwall	46	33
1991-92	Nottingham F	39	13
1992-93	Nottingham F	3	1
1992-93	Tottenham	38	21
1993-94	Tottenham	19	14
1994-95	Tottenham	42	18

Appearances

International: England (1993-) (6 apps, 0 goals), Youth.

PERSONAL FILE:

Full name: Edward Paul Sheringham.

Date of birth: April 2, 1966.

Birthplace: Highams Park, East London.

Family: I'm a policeman's son and have a brother Jim, who works in a bank and plays non-League football.

Nickname: Teddy. But my manager at Nottingham Forest, Brian Clough, insisted on calling me Edward. When I first joined he said: "That's the name on your birth certificate, isn't it?" No one had called me that since my mum when I was a little lad. I suppose it was his way of letting me know who was the boss.

Who was your boyhood hero? Glenn Hoddle, because of his pure class. I was an 11-year-old at Walthamstow's Chaple End Junior School when Liverpool won their first European Cup in 1977 so I also admired Kenny Dalglish. I idolised Trevor Brooking as well.

What has been your biggest thrill in life? Seeing my son, Charlie, born.

TEDDY SHERINGHAM

What has been your saddest moment in soccer?
Relegation from Division One with Millwall. We were a far better side than people gave us credit for and it was a terrible confidence knock for the club. I thought we would bounce back straight away.

Which present-day footballer do you admire most?
Paul Gascoigne. He can do things no other professional in the English game can do.

Who is the greatest player there has ever been? Diego Maradona, because he produced great moments when everybody was trying to stop him.

Who has been the greatest influence on your career?
Roger Cross, he was always giving me advice when I was a youngster at Millwall. I also owe a lot to George Graham. He might be wondering where he went wrong now I've become a £2-million player. When he was in charge at Millwall I was offered to Brentford for £5,000. And he loaned me to Aldershot and a club in Stockholm called Djurgardens. The other lads really thought he hated me. But being coached by him was one of the best things that could have happened to me. I dreamed of scoring from 30 yards out or bending the ball around the keeper. He told me the only thing that counts is getting the ball into the net as often as possible.

What has been your greatest sporting achievement outside football? Beating my Millwall colleagues, Ian Woan and Keith Stevens, in a game of golf in Hawaii. It made me the overall winner.

Have you ever been rejected by a club? Yes. I was turned down by Spurs, Crystal Palace and Leyton Orient as a kid.

Which teams did you support as a boy? West Ham, Spurs and Orient. I watched them all. And I used to love watching Liverpool and Dalglish when they were in town. I only ever dreamed I would be part of the top club scene myself.

Which is your favourite ground? Anfield, for its superb pitch and atmosphere. When I first played there in November 1988 I had never even been to Liverpool. I thought: 'This is it – the game you dream about when you're a kid.' I had so many butterflies when I walked out under the 'This Is Anfield' sign. Their fans really know what the game means.

TEDDY SHERINGHAM

Which is your least favourite ground? Selhurst Park.

What other sports and hobbies do you enjoy? Tennis, golf – and whatever my son wants to do at the time.

Who is your favourite sportsman outside football? Tennis star John McEnroe.

Who is your favourite manager? Brian Clough. When I first went to Forest I was really nervous. He had a reputation for bringing his big-money signings down to earth with a resounding thud. I'd heard about how Trevor Francis had to sweep the dressing-room floor and make the tea after becoming Britain's first £1 million player. But as it turned out he was a perfect gentleman.

Do you have any superstitions? I always put my right boot on first.

What are your most prized possessions? Medals for the Golden Boot in 90/91, the Second Division Championship with Millwall in 87/88 and Rumbelows Cup runners-up in 91/92. I also got great pleasure in breaking Derek Possee's goalscoring record at The Den.

Do you dream of a particular success in another sport? I'm quite happy trying to achieve my footballing dreams, which are difficult enough. I always wanted to play for England.

FAVOURITE FILE:

TV programme: *Only Fools And Horses.*

Pop star: Rod Stewart.

Food: Indian.

Drink: Budweiser.

Film: *The Deer Hunter.*

Film stars: Christopher Walken and Rachel Ward.

Holiday resort: Florida.

TV star: Ted Danson (of *Cheers).*

Comedian: Jasper Carrott.

CD: *Let's Get It On* by Marvin Gaye.

City: London.

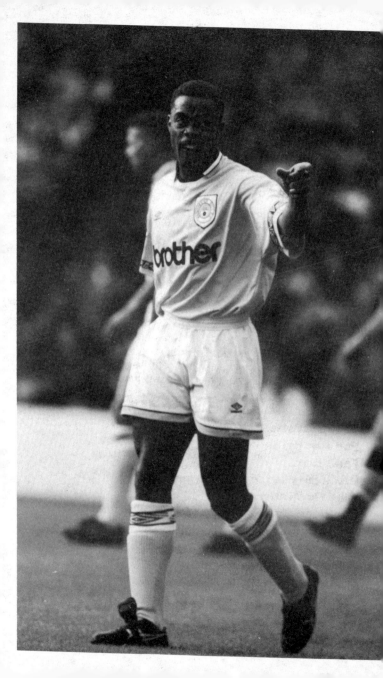

FITZROY SIMPSON

Season	Club	App	Goals
1988-89	Swindon Town	7	–
1989-90	Swindon Town	30	2
1990-91	Swindon Town	38	3
1991-92	Swindon Town	30	4
1991-92	Manchester City	11	1
1992-93	Manchester City	29	1
1993-94	Manchester City	15	–
1994-95	Manchester City	16	2

PERSONAL FILE:

Full name: Fitzroy Simpson.

Date of birth: February 26, 1970.

Birthplace: Bradford-On-Avon, Wiltshire.

Home: Four-bed detached house in Winslow, Cheshire.

Brothers and sisters: Two elder brothers: Melvin, who works for Avon Tyres, and Paul who works for Buxton Productions.

Father's job: My dad, Soloman, is a lorry driver.

Nickname: Simmo.

Who were your boyhood heroes? Glenn Hoddle and Pele.

What has been your biggest thrill in life? Playing football with Glenn Hoddle when we were at Swindon together.

What has been your biggest disappointment in life? The death of one of my dearest friends, Mr Allison.

What have been your best and worst moments in soccer? The best was when Swindon won promotion and the worst, 10 days later, when the League demoted us over the cash probe.

Which present-day footballer do you admire most? Gordon Strachan. His appetite and enthusiasm for the game is second to none. He's a great role model for younger players like myself.

What has been your greatest sporting achievement outside football? Beating my brothers and uncles at pool in our local pub.

FITZROY SIMPSON

Have you ever been rejected by a club? I was turned down by Manchester City when I was 12, and also by Bristol City when I was 15. They were tough decisions to take but I never lost faith in my ability and my friends and family encouraged me to keep going.

If you had a tattoo, what would it depict? I am too scared of those needles.

Who do you room with on away trips? Michel Vonk – his snoring is something terrible.

Who is the best trainer you have seen? My team-mate Paul Lake.

Which celebrity would make a good football manager? Claudia Schiffer. There's nothing the players would not do for her – even extra training.

What is the craziest request you have received from a fan? One asked me to autograph on her bikini line. I had to refuse – the wife would not have been too happy.

What would you be doing if you weren't a footballer? Hopefully something which pays lots of cash – like a golfer or boxer.

Have you ever needed a kick up the backside in football? I've had loads of kicks up the backside from all my managers. Why? I keep asking myself. None of them explained why.

Which team did you support as a boy? If I told the truth, Manchester City fans would kill me – so I'll say Exeter City!

How would you describe yourself for a lonely hearts ad? Young, married, good-looking, interesting, understanding – but, when replying, try getting past the wife.

What hobbies do you enjoy? Gardening.

Who or what irritates you most in football? Doing shadow play when preparing for the opposition. It bores me to death.

Do you have any superstitions? I like to go out on to the pitch in third spot.

Do you dream of a particular success in another sport? To become the heavyweight champion of the world.

FITZROY SIMPSON

Pop star: Luther Vandross.
Food: Rice and chicken.
Drink: Lager, wine.
Film: *Coming To America*.
Film star: Eddie Murphy.
Holiday spot: Greek islands, Jamaica.
Comedian: Lenny Henry.
Sports star: Mike Tyson.
CD: *The Very Best Of Luther Vandross*.
Soap opera: *Home And Away*.
Soap character: Tug.

MARK HATELEY

Season	Club	Lge App	Lge Goals
1978-79	Coventry	1	–
1979-80	Coventry	4	–
1980-81	Coventry	19	3
1981-82	Coventry	34	13
1982-83	Coventry	35	9
1983-84	Portsmouth	38	22
1984-85	AC Milan	21	7
1985-86	AC Milan	22	8
1986-87	AC Milan	23	2
1987-90	To Monaco		
1990-91	Glasgow Rangers	33	10
1991-92	Glasgow Rangers	30	21
1992-93	Glasgow Rangers	37	19
1993-94	Glasgow Rangers	42	22
1994-95	Glasgow Rangers	23	13

Appearances

International: England (1984-) (32 apps, 9 goals), Youth, U21.

PERSONAL FILE:

Full name: Mark Wayne Hateley.

Date of birth: November 7, 1961.

Birthplace: Liverpool.

Father's job: My dad Tony was a professional footballer, now he's a brewery rep. My dad played for Notts County, Villa, Chelsea, Liverpool, Coventry, Birmingham and Oldham.

Brothers and sisters: A younger sister, Tina.

Family pets: A labrador, Sam, and a bulldog, Jock. Plus five tropical fish!

Nickname: Hates.

Who was your boyhood hero? I was too busy playing to watch other people and have heroes.

What has been your biggest thrill in life? Recovering from the knee injury I had at Monaco and signing for Rangers.

What has been your biggest disappointment? Getting that injury. I challenged for the ball with a goalkeeper and my

MARK HATELEY

foot got stuck in a hole in the ground. While my foot went one way the keeper clattered into me and sent my knee the other. It was gruesome.

What is your saddest moment in soccer? Any Saturday when we've lost.

Which present-day footballer do you admire most? Roberto Baggio of Juventus, for his all-round ability.

Who would you pick as your greatest player? Zico of Brazil, who was deadly from anywhere in the opposition's half.

Who are your favourite sportsmen outside football? Nigel Mansell and Barry Sheene.

What is the best part of your job? The banter at training.

What is the worst? Injuries.

Who has been the biggest influence on your career? My dad, Tony.

What has been your greatest game? Luckily, I've been involved in too many to single out one.

What has been your most memorable goal? I enjoy them all but the equaliser in our 2-2 draw with Marseilles at Ibrox was probably the most important one I've ever scored.

Who has been your toughest opponent? Claudio Gentile of Juventus.

What has been your biggest regret in football? Missing so much of my career through injury and, particularly, missing out on the 1990 World Cup finals.

Would you like to be a manager? You never know!

What would you be doing if you weren't a footballer? I'd probably be a cricketer or a rugby player because I was good at both at school.

Who would you most like to be? Nigel Mansell.

Have you ever been rejected by a club? Nottingham Forest. Brian Clough told me I'd *never* be a player.

What is your worst fault? I always get grumpy on a Friday.

Which team did you support as a boy? Nottingham Forest.

Which is your favourite ground? The Azteca Stadium in Mexico.

MARK HATELEY

Which is your least favourite ground? I can't say, otherwise the Scottish Football Association would fine me!

What other sports do you enjoy? Tennis and golf, but I rarely have the time.

What luxury item would you take to a desert island? An endless supply of Marks and Spencer's food.

What is your ideal evening out? A meal and a few drinks with friends.

What is the most dangerous thing you've ever done? Drive a powerboat at 115mph over a choppy sea at Viareggio. It was hair-raising but exhilarating.

What dangerous thing would you most like to attempt? Formula one racing, which looks like me driving to work every morning.

What is the most embarrassing thing that's ever happened to you? Being nutmegged by Gary Stevens.

What are your most prized possessions? My cars.

Who would you most like to meet? Actor Robert De Niro.

What job would you like after you stop playing? Deckchair attendant at Bondi Beach.

FAVOURITE FILE:

TV programme: *A Question Of Sport.*
Pop star: Billy Idol.
Food: Anything.
Drink: Milk.
Film: *Scent Of A Woman.*
Film star: Al Pacino, Robert De Niro.
Animal: Dog.
Holiday resort: Barbados.
Comedian: Chubby Brown.
Single: 'Jump' by Van Halen.
CD: *Idol Hits* by Billy Idol.
City: Florence.
Soap opera: *Neighbours.*
Soap character: Bouncer the dog.

GARY SPEED

Season	Club	Lge App	Lge Goals
1988-89	Leeds	1	–
1989-90	Leeds	25	3
1990-91	Leeds	38	7
1991-92	Leeds	41	7
1992-93	Leeds	39	7
1993-94	Leeds	36	10
1994-95	Leeds	38	3

Appearances

International: Wales (1990) (31 apps, 1 goal), U21.

PERSONAL FILE:

Full name: Gary Andrew Speed.

Date of birth: September 8, 1969.

Birthplace: Mancot in North Wales.

Father's job: Roger is a fireman.

Brothers and sisters: One sister, Lesley, who is an air stewardess for British Airways.

Nickname: Speedo and Speedy.

What was your childhood ambition? To be a top footballer.

Who was your boyhood hero? Pele. He was without doubt the best.

What has been your biggest thrill in life? Winning the Division One title in 1992. It was just unbelievable the way it happened. Manchester United looked to have it in the bag but then we crept up on them and won it.

What has been your biggest disappointment? When I was rejected by the Wales schoolboys team. I went for a trial at Aberystwyth and, when I wasn't picked, I thought: 'That's it – I'm never going to make a professional footballer now.'

Which present-day footballer do you admire most? John Barnes. He's the British footballer with the most ability.

Who has been the greatest influence on your career? My dad, Roger. He has followed, supported and helped me since I was very young.

G A R Y   S P E E D

What can you remember of your first goal for Leeds?
It was at Elland Road against Bradford City. John Hendrie flicked
on a long throw from Vinny Jones and I hit it on the half-volley
and it went in. That put us ahead but the night was spoiled in a
way because we needed the three points and they equalised with
a disputed penalty in the last five minutes.

**What are the most important goals you have scored
for Leeds?** The goal I scored against Stuttgart in the European
Cup at Elland Road stands out, we had lost the first leg 3-0 and
that was the early goal we needed to put us back into contention.
My goal against Sheffield United in the Second Division
promotion season stands out too. Both teams were level on
points at the top and we beat them 4-0 at Elland Road.

Who has been your toughest opponent? It has to be
Liverpool and Denmark midfielder Jan Molby. The big man just
never gives the ball away.

What would you be doing if you weren't a footballer?
I really don't know, this was all I ever wanted to do.

**What has been your greatest sporting achievement
outside football?** Playing cricket for the Wales schoolboys
side for two years when I was 12 and 13. I was a bit of an all-
rounder but I never did anything special – except for one knock
of 48.

Have you ever been rejected by a club? Manchester City
rejected me at 15. It knocked my confidence but, fortunately for
me, everything worked out fine at Leeds.

Which is your favourite ground? Apart from Elland Road,
I would choose Goodison Park – a great stadium with a great
pitch and the Leeds fans always make it a superb atmosphere
there.

Which team did you support as a boy? Everton.

What other sports do you enjoy? When I get the time,
I love to play a round of golf.

Who are your favourite sportsmen outside football?
Cricketer Ian Botham and golfer Ian Woosnam. They are both
fighters and winners.

Do you have any superstitions? Only not to have
superstitions.

GARY SPEED

What is your most prized possession? My Division One championship medal.

TV programme: *Cheers.*
Food: Italian.
Drink: Lager.
Film: *The Deer Hunter.*
Film star: Robert De Niro.
Holiday resort: Greece.
TV star: Ted Danson.
Comedians: Eddie Murphy, Harry Enfield.
City: Leeds.
Soap opera: *Coronation Street.*
Soap characters: Reg Holdsworth, Vera Duckworth.

ALAN KELLY

Season	Club	Lge App	Lge Goals
1985-86	Preston NE	13	–
1986-87	Preston NE	22	–
1987-88	Preston NE	19	–
1988-89	Preston NE	–	–
1989-90	Preston NE	42	–
1990-91	Preston NE	23	–
1991-92	Preston NE	23	–
1992-93	Sheffield United	33	–
1993-94	Sheffield United	30	–
1994-95	Sheffield United	38	–

Appearances

International: Rep of Ireland (1993-) (3 apps, 0 goals), Youth, U21.

PERSONAL FILE:

Full name: Alan Thomas Kelly.

Date of birth: August 11, 1968.

Birthplace: Preston.

Home: A converted coach-house in the Derbyshire Peak District.

Brothers and sisters: Two older brothers: David, who works for British Aerospace, and Gary, who is a professional goalkeeper.

Father's job: My dad, Alan, owns the Corner Kick soccer centre in Maryland, USA.

Family pets: A Great Dane called Hattie.

Nickname: Ned.

What was your childhood ambition? To be an astronaut or stuntman.

Who was your boyhood hero? George Best, because the ball seemed to be stuck to his feet.

What has been your biggest thrill in life? Playing at Wembley, playing for the Republic of Ireland and getting married.

A L A N K E L L Y

What has been your biggest disappointment? Being knocked down by a motorbike as I crossed the road to get a new pair of gloves from a sports shop. It meant 18 months out of the game – I never did get those gloves.

What has been your saddest moment in soccer? Hillsborough, the Bradford fire disaster, and the death of my good friend, Mick Baxter, who was with Preston, Middlesbrough and Portsmouth.

Which present-day footballer do you admire most? My former Sheffield United team-mate, Alan Cork. If I had a contract like his at his age I'd be well happy.

Who would you pick as your greatest player? Neville Southall. At his best, he was unbeatable.

Who has been the greatest influence on your career? My father, Alan, because he has been there, seen it and done it. He was the Republic's goalkeeper for 11 years, winning 47 caps. In 1964 he kept goal for Preston in their FA Cup Final defeat by West Ham. Another big influence was former Preston goalkeeper Roy Tunks, who played more than 600 games.

Did your father want you to follow in his footsteps? Dad came out with all the sensible reasons for not turning professional, that I should finish my four-year apprenticeship. But my mind was made up.

Who is your toughest opponent? Ian Wright – he makes you expect the unexpected.

What would you be doing if you weren't a footballer? I was an apprentice electrician for 15 months before I joined Preston so I suppose I would still be a sparky.

What is your greatest sporting achievement outside football? I broke the Lancashire county record at high jump.

What is your funniest moment on the pitch? When my Sheffield United team-mate Paul Beesley lay injured on the ground chewing clumps of grass. He insisted it eased the pain.

What is the oddest training you have ever done? Paintball, Army games and go-karting with Dave Bassett.

Which team did you support as a boy? Preston North End. My dad was there for 30 years so I had no choice.

A L A N   K E L L Y

Which are your favourite grounds? Wembley, Anfield and Old Trafford – grounds where legends played.

What other sports and hobbies do you enjoy? A hack around a golf course, and walking the dog.

Is there an unusual food that improves your game? My mother-in-law's chocolate parcels.

Who is your favourite sportsman outside football? England rugby skipper Bill Beaumont was an inspirational leader with a down-to-earth personality who is greatly respected.

Who is your favourite manager? Tommy Booth and Brian Kidd. They took the gamble to sign me professionally and gave me my debut at 17.

What is your most prized possession? My health and my family.

Do you play any musical instruments? I try to play the drums.

Do you dream of a particular success in another sport? Winning the high-jump gold medal at the Olympic Games.

FAVOURITE FILE:

TV programme: *Cheers*.

Pop star: U2.

Food: Pasta.

Drink: Tea, lager.

Film: *The Deer Hunter*.

Film stars: Clint Eastwood, Demi Moore.

Holiday resort: Antigua.

TV star: Norm in *Cheers*.

Comedian: Robin Williams.

CD: U2's *Joshua Tree*.

Cities: Sheffield, Dublin.

Soap: *Emmerdale, Brookside*.

Soap character: Sinbad.

CHRIS KIWOMYA

Season	Club	Lge App	Lge Goals
1986-87	Ipswich	–	–
1987-88	Ipswich	–	–
1988-89	Ipswich	26	2
1989-90	Ipswich	29	5
1990-91	Ipswich	37	10
1991-92	Ipswich	43	16
1992-93	Ipswich	38	10
1993-94	Ipswich	37	5
1994-95	Ipswich	11	3
1994-95	Arsenal	15	3

PERSONAL FILE:

Full name: Chris Kiwomya.

Date of birth: December 2, 1969.

Birthplace: Huddersfield.

Father's job: My dad, Sam, is a doctor in Antigua. My parents are divorced. My mother, Curlyn, is a midwife in Bradford.

Brothers and sisters: Four brothers – Adrian, Paul, Andrew and Nicholas – and one sister, Andrea.

Nickname: Lino or Benson. My old Ipswich boss, John Lyall, first called me Lino because he said I was always falling on the floor in training.

What has been your biggest thrill in life? Scoring my first goal for Ipswich.

What has been your biggest disappointment? The death of my grandparents. They lived in Jamaica.

What has been your saddest moment in soccer? When my brother Andrew, who played for Barnsley and Sheffield Wednesday, had to quit because of an injured back. He was only 21.

Which present-day footballer do you admire most? Ruud Gullit – he has pace, power and skill.

Who would you pick as your greatest player? Pele. I have watched soccer videos of him for hours.

CHRIS KIWOMYA

Who has been the biggest influence on your career?
My mum for all her support. She was the Jamaican all-island sprint champion before she came to England. She could still beat me over 100 yards when I was 14. It was so embarrassing that I didn't dare tell anyone at school.

Who has been your toughest opponent? Des Walker. He let me out of his pocket at the end of the game.

If you won a million, what would you buy first? A big, fat mansion in Beverley Hills.

Who would you most like to be? Basketball star Michael Jordan. He's brilliant. I've seen him play several times in America.

What is the oddest training you've ever done? Forty footballers playing rugby in the indoor gym at Ipswich. It was John Lyall's idea for a bit of light relief. Everyone enjoyed it.

Which team did you support as a boy? Bradford City. I had trials with various Yorkshire clubs and could have joined a local club. But I had no hesitation in going to Ipswich because the facilities and atmosphere were so impressive.

Which is your favourite ground? Elland Road – the fans are so quiet there!

What other sports and hobbies do you enjoy? Tennis, badminton and listening to music.

What has been your greatest sporting achievement outside football? I was the Bradford schools champion at 1,500 metres – I have to admit I never really liked the sprints.

What dangerous thing would you most like to attempt? Skydiving.

What is the biggest drawback about being a professional footballer? Having to play over Christmas and the New Year.

What is your most prized possession? A ring given to me by my mother on my 16th birthday. I put tape over it before every game.

Who would you most like to meet? The Pope.

Who is your favourite manager? John Lyall. He's as honest as the day is long. He put in a lot of time and effort to help me

CHRIS KIWOMYA

with my game. I used to go back to the ground for extra training in the afternoon and have a friendly chat with him. We talked about football, sport, politics and life generally. The boss was always there to help me. I shall always be grateful.

Which world figure do you most admire and why? The US President George Bush, for his stand in the Gulf War.

FAVOURITE FILE:

TV programme: *The Cosby Show.*
Pop star: Barry White.
Food: My mum's Jamaican rice, peas and chicken.
Drink: Lucozade.
Film: *Boyz N The Hood.*
Film star: Eddie Murphy.
Holiday spot: Vancouver.
TV star: Bill Cosby.
Comedian: Benny Hill.
Single: Randy Crawford's 'Rainy Night In Georgia'.
CD: Loose Ends' *Look How Long.*
City: Los Angeles.
Soap opera: *EastEnders.*

KENNY SANSOM

Season	Club	Lge App	Lge Goals
1974-75	Crystal Palace	1	–
1975-76	Crystal Palace	6	–
1976-77	Crystal Palace	46	–
1977-78	Crystal Palace	41	2
1978-79	Crystal Palace	42	–
1979-80	Crystal Palace	36	1
1980-81	Arsenal	42	3
1981-82	Arsenal	42	–
1982-83	Arsenal	40	–
1983-84	Arsenal	40	1
1984-85	Arsenal	39	1
1985-86	Arsenal	42	–
1986-87	Arsenal	35	–
1987-88	Arsenal	34	1
1988-89	Arsenal	–	–
1988-89	Newcastle	20	–
1989-90	QPR	36	–
1990-91	QPR	28	–
1990-91	Coventry	9	–
1991-92	Coventry	21	–
1992-93	Coventry	21	–
1992-93	Everton	7	1
1992-93	Brentford	8	–

Appearances

International: England (1979-88) (86 apps, 1 goal), Schools, Youth, U21, England B, Football League.

Full name: Kenneth George Sansom.

Date of birth: September 26, 1958.

Birthplace: London.

Brothers and sisters: Three sisters: Margaret, Maureen and Mary – and two brothers: Peter and David.

Family pets: My daughter, Katie, has a budgie called George.

Nickname: I was called Five Bellies when I was out injured and put on some weight!

KENNY SANSOM

Who were your boyhood heroes? England keeper Gordon
Banks and left-back Terry Cooper. I used to be a goalkeeper till
I was 12. Unfortunately, the goals got bigger and I didn't.

What have been your most thrilling moments? In life,
the birth of my children. In soccer, my England debut against
Wales in 1979 – and when I scored against Finland at Wembley.
Bobby Robson had told me five minutes before that we needed
another goal. Lo and behold, I hit a screamer.

What has been your biggest disappointment in life?
Not staying at Arsenal for the rest of my career. They are a
fantastic club.

What has been your saddest moment in soccer? Luton
beating Arsenal in the League Cup final – and Diego Maradona's
'Hand of God' goal in the Mexico World Cup semi-finals. I have
an 8ft by 4ft picture of him handling the ball. I'm thinking of
hanging it in the loo.

Which present-day footballer do you admire most? Ray
Wilkins. He never gives the ball away and works very hard. He
enjoys it so much that it rubs off on everybody.

Who would you pick as your greatest player? Johan
Cruyff – although I never saw much of George Best.

Who has been the biggest influence on your career?
My mum, Rose. When I was young I was training with QPR
and found it hard to cope with the long journey home in the dark
from Ruislip to Camberwell in south London. My mum told me to
give it one last try and, if I still felt miserable, to pack it in. When
I came out of the Ruislip training ground that night and walked on
my own to the station, I made up my mind that I was finished
with football. It wasn't worth the misery. As I turned into the
station entrance, there was my mum, standing there waiting to
keep me company. And she was there every night after that, as
well. They say there's always a moment of inspiration in any
man's success story. Believe me, that was mine. She has backed
me all the way, watching as many games as possible. She even
went to Holland when I played for England schoolboys.

Who was your toughest opponent? Blackburn's Noel
Brotherston. When I was a kid of about 20, he tore me apart for
the first 45 minutes.

Have you ever been rejected by a club? No, as an

KENNY SANSOM

England schoolboy, you have lots of clubs looking at you. I could have joined Brian Clough at Leeds, as well as Villa and Spurs. I chose Crystal Palace because they were in the Third and I wanted first-team football as soon as possible.

Who is the funniest player you have known? My QPR team-mate Alan McDonald. He loves a joke and they're still funny even when he repeats them!

Which team did you support as a boy? Chelsea. I got the idea for long throw-ins from Ian Hutchinson.

What other sports do you enjoy? Tennis and snooker. My best break is 45. I once played Steve Davis – I only potted one yellow! He's a genius and a smashing bloke.

Who is your favourite sportsman outside football? US golfer, Fred Couples – although, of course, I want our British blokes to beat him.

What are your most prized possessions? My family, my 86 England caps and my schoolboy cap. I played about 10 times but you only get one cap. My mum has that.

Do you play any musical instruments? My wife gave me a guitar. I can strum a bit and sing 'Running Bear'. I might try and learn a bit more when I get older and get the rocking chair out.

Who are your favourite football managers? Terry Venables is a terrific coach – so bright. And I liked working for Jim Smith – he's great fun.

FAVOURITE FILE:

TV programme: *Only Fools And Horses.*
Pop stars: Johnny Mathis and Shirley Bassey.
Food: Chips.
Drink: White wine.
Films: *The Sting* and *Ghost.*
Film stars: Steve McQueen, Paul Newman.
Resort: Clearwater, Florida.
TV star: David Jason.
Comedian: Tommy Cooper.
Single: 'Goodnight Girl' by Wet Wet Wet.
City: London.

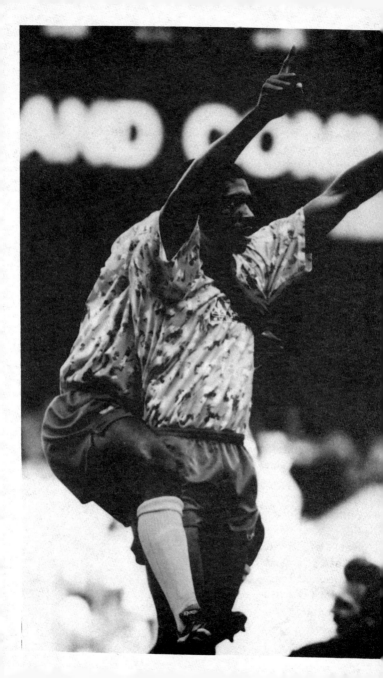

EFAN EKOKU

Season	Club	Lge App	Lge Goals
1990-91	Bournemouth	20	3
1991-92	Bournemouth	28	11
1992-93	Bournemouth	14	7
1992-93	Norwich	4	3
1993-94	Norwich	27	12
1994-95	Norwich	6	0
1994-95	Wimbledon	25	9

Appearances
International: Nigeria (1994-) (6 apps, 0 goals).

PERSONAL FILE:

Full name: Efan Ekoku.

Date of birth: June 8, 1967.

Birthplace: Manchester.

Brothers and sisters: Three brothers – Chuck is a fitness instructor; Abi was the UK discus champion but is now a professional Rugby League player for the London Broncos; and Uko plays semi-professional football.

Father's job: My dad, Clifford, is a property developer.

Nickname: Chief.

Who was your boyhood hero? I had two – George Best and Kevin Keegan.

What was your biggest thrill in life? Making my international debut for Nigeria against Zaire.

What has been your biggest disappointment? Not playing in the 1994 World Cup Finals. I went to America with the Nigerian squad but never got a game.

What have been your best and worst moments in soccer? The best was becoming the first player to score four goals in one Premiership game – for Norwich against Everton. The worst was an ankle injury during my Bournemouth days. Two operations kept me out for more than a year.

Which present-day footballers do you admire most? Mark Hughes, for his superb all-round game, and Ian Rush, the deadliest finisher of the 80's.

EFAN EKOKU

Who would you pick as your greatest player? The greatest I have seen is Diego Maradona. He had the all-round ability to create goals, score goals and lead teams inspirationally at the highest level.

What has been your greatest sporting achievement outside football? I was the Under-16 Merseyside long jump champion. I also played rugby for Liverpool College and the Lancashire Under-16 squad.

If you had a tattoo, what would it depict? I would have the green eagle of Nigeria on my left breast. My dad took the family back to Nigeria from Liverpool when I was 16. I didn't play football for six years because I was going through college and earning money in a double-glazing firm. But my brother, Abi, said I was wasting my talent so I went to non-League Sutton for a trial. They took me on after a few weeks and I immediately gave up the double glazing because I wanted to be a professional footballer.

Who do you room with on away trips? Alan Reeves – I cannot understand a word he says.

Who has been the greatest influence on your career? My dad, for his continuous support and criticism; and Keith Blunt, for improving my all-round game.

Who is the best trainer you have seen? Jimmy Case, during my Bournemouth days. Even in his late 30's, he was never late for training, encouraged the younger players and always gave 100 per cent in matches.

Have you ever been mistaken for someone else? Yes, pop star Keith Sweat.

What would you be doing if you weren't a footballer? I'd be an athlete or tennis player.

Have you ever needed a kick up the backside in football? Yes, from my Bournemouth boss, Tony Pulis.

Which team did you support as a boy? Liverpool, where I was brought up.

How would you describe yourself for a lonely hearts ad? Attached.

What other sports and hobbies do you enjoy? Tennis, snooker and winding other people up.

E F A N   E K O K U

What is your most prized possession? My feet.

Do you dream of a particular success in another sport?
I would like to win the Olympic 100-metres gold medal.

FAVOURITE FILE:

TV programme: *Roseanne.*

Pop stars: En Vogue, Luther Vandross.

Food: Roast chicken, rice and plantain.

Drink: Blackcurrant and water.

Film: *Godfather* trilogy.

Film stars: Al Pacino, Meryl Streep.

Holiday spot: Nigeria.

TV star: Leonard Rossiter.

Comedian: Harry Enfield.

Sports star: Muhammad Ali.

City: Liverpool.

Soap operas: *Brookside, Coronation Street.*

Soap character: Roseanne Barr.

T O N Y   G A L E

Season	Club	Lge App	Lge Goals
1977-78	Fulham	38	8
1978-79	Fulham	36	2
1979-80	Fulham	42	4
1980-81	Fulham	40	1
1981-82	Fulham	44	1
1982-83	Fulham	42	2
1983-84	Fulham	35	1
1984-85	West Ham	37	–
1985-86	West Ham	42	–
1986-87	West Ham	32	2
1987-88	West Ham	18	–
1988-89	West Ham	31	–
1989-90	West Ham	36	1
1990-91	West Ham	24	1
1991-92	West Ham	25	–
1992-93	West Ham	23	1
1993-94	West Ham	32	–
1994-95	Blackburn	15	–

Appearances

International: England Youth, U21.

PERSONAL FILE:

Full name: Anthony Peter Gale.

Date of birth: November 19, 1959.

Birthplace: Westminster.

Parents: My dad, Peter, is a London taxi driver; my mum, Valerie is a civil servant.

Brothers and sisters: A younger sister, Joanne, who is a housewife.

Nickname: Galey or Old Man.

What has been your biggest thrill in life? Being at the birth of my two children. We had a tough two weeks after my daughter, Alexandra, was born with a virus. She had to be starved to get rid of it and, for a while, it was touch and go whether she would be all right.

What has been your biggest disappointment? Leaving

two great clubs in Fulham and West Ham. I also thoroughly enjoyed my year at Blackburn.

What have been your best and worst moments in soccer? The worst was in my West Ham days when I was sent off in the FA Cup semi-final against Forest. The best was getting the chance to play at Blackburn.

Who was your boyhood hero? Peter Osgood – I was a Chelsea supporter as a kid.

What is your greatest sporting achievement outside football? A hole-in-one at Richmond Golf Club when I was playing with my Uncle Terry. It was a 120-yard par-three hole uphill to a blind green. I used a nine-iron and, when we got to the green, I could not find my ball. We looked around the green and in the bunkers. I said to my uncle: 'I can't believe I've lost it – I hit it perfectly.' I finally looked in the hole and there it was – brilliant!

Who do you room with on away trips? Chris Sutton. He's very untidy, leaving a trail of destruction everywhere.

Who is the best trainer you have seen — and the worst? The worst in my opinion, was Frank McAvennie, but, come Saturday, he was brilliant. The best is Ludek Miklosko – a superb athlete and a great footballer.

Have you ever been mistaken for someone else? Yes, Tony Cascarino. I am not sure if that's a compliment to him or me.

Which celebrity would make a good football manager? Richard Digance – he knows nothing about football but you would have no time to get nervous as he would have you falling about laughing.

What is the craziest request you've had from a fan? To sign parts of the body my wife would not approve of.

Have you ever needed a kick up the backside in football? The people who are closest to me are normally very honest about my play. So I'm kicked before I am kicked professionally.

Which team did you support as a boy? Chelsea – my favourites were Alan Hudson and Peter Osgood.

What TV show would you most like to be in? I would love

to have been in *Only Fools And Horses* or *Tiswas*. Both shows looked great fun with plenty of ad-libbing.

How would you describe yourself for a lonely hearts ad? 35, going grey rapidly, no co-ordination on the dance floor. But I'm sure if you look hard enough there must be something going for me.

What other sports do you enjoy? Golf, swimming and watching live cricket. My golf handicap is 16 – but I play off 20 if it's for money!

Do you have any superstitions? I go on the pitch 30 minutes before the game to warm up – always with my wristwatch on. I go back into the dressing room exactly 15 minutes before kick-off and, exactly 10 minutes before kick-off, I remove my watch.

What is your most prized possession? A trunkful of cuttings and photographs of my career. My mum has all my medals and my England Youth and U-21 caps – she won't let me near them.

FAVOURITE FILE:

TV programme: *Cracker*.

Pop stars: Alison Moyet, Paul Young, Tony Hadley.

Food: Grilled chicken and pasta.

Drink: Dry white wine.

Film: *The Magnificent Seven*.

Film stars: James Woods, Tommy Lee Jones.

Holiday spot: Marbella.

TV star: Robbie Coltrane.

Comedian: Bernard Manning.

Sports star: Nick Faldo.

CD: *Louis Armstrong*.

City: London.

Soap opera: *Brookside*.

Soap character: Sinbad.

P H I L   B A B B

CAREER RECORD:

Season	Club	Lge App	Lge Goals
1988-89	Millwall	–	–
1989-90	Millwall	–	–
1990-91	Bradford C	34	10
1991-92	Bradford	46	4
1992-93	Coventry C	34	–
1993-94	Coventry	40	3
1994-95	Liverpool	33	0

Appearances

International: Rep of Ireland (1994-) (14 apps, 0 goals).

PERSONAL FILE:

Full name: Phil Andrew Babb.

Date of birth: November 30, 1970.

Birthplace: Lambeth.

Brothers and sisters: An older brother, Robert, and a sister, Marie.

Family pets: A puppy called Boots.

Nickname: Babbsy.

What was your childhood ambition? Simply to have a stress-free life and enjoy it.

Who was your boyhood hero? Michel Platini, a classy player with great vision who scored super goals.

Your saddest moment in soccer? When Millwall sacked manager John Docherty. He got them promotion to the First Division and, when things looked bad, he wasn't given the chance to sort it out.

Which present day footballer do you admire most? 'Sir' Glenn Hoddle – a true talent who plays the game with flair and grace. He still has a passion for the way the game should be played.

Who would you pick as your greatest player? I can't answer-there have been too many great players over the years each with something special. I could not split Pele, Cruyff, Platini, Maradona or John Williams!

P H I L B A B B

Who has been the greatest influence on your career?
My brother-in-law, George, because we spent endless days
over the park playing. It made me love the game.

Who has been your toughest opponent? Eric Cantona is
not so much the toughest as the most awkward. He drifts deep
into positions that make defenders think twice about marking
him.

What would you be doing if you weren't a footballer?
I would like to have been a journalist. I was already enrolled for a
course in journalism in south London when a Millwall scout
watched me. Just think, if he had had a cold that day and not
turned up, I might be nowhere now.

Have you ever been rejected by a club? No. Millwall
spotted me at school and offered me an apprenticeship.

What has been your funniest moment on the pitch?
During shooting training at Coventry, keeper Steve Ogrizovic
tried to catch a ball heading straight for his face. Suddenly he
moved his hands and it smashed into Oggy's face knocking him
over. The rest of us were floored with laughter.

What is the oddest of training you've ever done? At
Coventry every Mick Brown and Phil Neal training session was
odd.

Which team did you support as a boy? I wasn't that
interested in football as a kid. I've always liked Spurs *and*
Arsenal, plus the early 1980s French side.

Which is your favourite ground? Lansdowne Road. When
I made my debut for the Republic of Ireland the reception I got
was amazing. I'll never forget it.

Which is your least favourite? Loftus Road.

What other sports do you enjoy? Basketball, tennis and
I also play computer games.

Do you play any musical instruments? I have a keyboard
that I play about with but I would like to have piano lessons.

**Do you ever dream of a particular success in another
sport?** To be the first black player since Arthur Ashe to win the
Wimbledon men's title.

P H I L B A B B

Which world figure do you most admire? Any person who is kind-hearted and does some good in the world gets my vote.

FAVOURITE FILE:

TV programme: *Fresh Prince Of Bel Air.*

Drink: Black Velvet (Champagne and Guinness).

Film: *Less Than Zero.*

Film stars: Harrison Ford, Val Kilmer.

Animal: Polar bear.

Holiday resort: A holiday would be nice.

City: London.

Soap opera: *Coronation Street.*

Soap character: Jack Duckworth.